DIFF...

BATTLES

The Search for a World War II Hero

DIFFERENT BATTLES

The Search for a World War II Hero

by
Rody Johnson

Sunflower University Press®

1531 Yuma • P. O. Box 1009 • Manhattan, Kansas 66505-1009 USA

Edited by Sonie Liebler

Layout by Lori L. Daniel

ISBN 0-89745-236-4

Sunflower University Press is a wholly-owned subsidiary
of the non-profit 501(c)3 Journal of the West, Inc.

To Katharine

"Whee!" yelled the little fishies, "Here's a lot of fun,
We'll swim in the sea till the day is done."
They swam and they swam and it was a lark.
Till all of a sudden they met a SHARK.

> — From the 1939 hit song, "Three Little Fishies,"
> the inspiration for the insignia on the conning
> tower of *U-333*, a World War II German subma-
> rine, commanded by Peter Cremer.

Contents

List of Illustrations

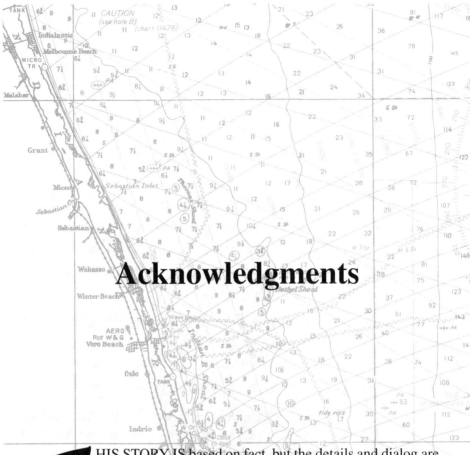

Acknowledgments

*T*HIS STORY IS based on fact, but the details and dialog are imagined for some of the events that took place during the war.

Nancy Hopkins, a teacher and artist, convinced me I could write this story and then pulled it out of me bit by bit over four years.

Kay Odekirk at the Center for the Arts in Vero Beach and Ken Smith at the University of Tennessee-Chattanooga taught me some writing fundamentals. Captain Arthur Moore, who self-published his monumental book that documented Merchant Marine losses in World War II, provided the information about the American tanker *Java Arrow*. Philip Neal, retired Superintendent of the Mobil tanker fleet, added details. The German Commander Peter Cremer sent me naval reports and photographs from his personal archives. Mark Mondano shared his copies of U-boat war logs that he had obtained from the National Archives. Herb Spitler, a former World War II German airman, translated portions of the *U-333* and *U-109* logs pertinent to the operations of those two submarines off Florida.

Descriptions of Peter Cremer's war adventures are based on his book, *U-boat Commander*, and my conversations with him in Reinbek, Germany. His Paris party and dinner with German Admiral Karl Doenitz are based on pieces from Jean Noli's *The Admiral's Wolfpack*.

Wayne Harkness, a U.S. Naval Academy graduate, who commanded destroyers during World War II on anti-submarine patrol in both the Atlantic and the Pacific Oceans, reviewed the book for nautical and naval accuracy.

My thanks go to readers Betty Jean Hensick, Sharon Sexton, Woody Rowe, Mark Johnson, Buck Johnson, Bill Leesman, Lisa Angel, Cricket Peckstein, Marilyn Chenault, John Stillwell, and Katharine Johnson, all of whom gave me useful suggestions.

During a stay at the Vermont Studio School, I worked with Al Young and Shelby Herron who helped establish the story's basic structure. Dorian Hastings added copy editing advice. Charlotte Morgan and Sonie Liebler provided the final refinements.

The Hal Leonard Corporation, Milwaukee, Wisconsin, has graciously allowed the reprinting of a portion of the lyrics from "Three Little Fishies (Itty Bitty Poo)." Words and Music by Saxie Dowell, Copyright © 1939 by Chappell & Co., Copyright Renewed. International Copyright Secured. All Rights Reserved.

Chapter 1

Bethel Shoal
May 5, 1942

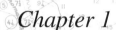

ETHEL SHOAL lies submerged seven miles off the Florida East Coast just to the northeast of Vero Beach. This mile-long, uneven sand bar runs southwest to northeast and is covered by 30 feet of water. A buoy is anchored at the shoal's northeast edge. Its light, a gas-lit flame, blinks on and off at set intervals. Seaward from the buoy the water depth drops rapidly to 90 feet. Ten miles farther out, the Gulf Stream meanders northward.

On a warm evening, a southeast breeze pushed a two-foot sea that rolled gently over the shoal. In the darkness, the mainland glowed as lights from the small towns along the coast reflected against white puffy clouds that hung over the shoreline.

In the deeper water 300 yards east of the buoy, a 200-foot German submarine rose from the bottom as it prepared to surface. The U-boat had arrived the previous night after a 4,000-mile, 36-day trip across the Atlantic — destination: the Bethel Shoal buoy. Its mission was to fire its 17 torpedoes to sink U.S. and Allied shipping. The submarine, designated *U-333*, carried a crew of 55 and was commanded by Peter Cremer, a bearded, 31-year-old graduate of the German Naval Academy.

The sub's conning tower broke the surface in a swirl of phosphorous-streaked foam. Cremer and four lookouts scrambled onto the bridge and each quickly scanned his assigned quarter of the compass. Cremer searched the surface with his binoculars, then looked skyward seeking signs of enemy activity. The sea lay quiet. He dropped his binoculars, letting them hang around his neck, and glanced at the buoy as it blinked and at the lights of the coast beyond. "These Americans," he said to the lookout standing on the starboard side, "they don't know that they are at war!"

Several miles north of Bethel Shoal, the USS *Java Arrow*, a 20-year-old American tanker owned by Socony Vacuum Oil, plodded southward, unescorted, hugging the coastline, following the ten-fathom (60-foot depth) curve per Navy instructions. She moved at ten knots without lights. The tanker was in ballast — carrying no cargo, but her tanks were filled with water for stability — headed from New York to a refinery in the Netherlands Antilles in the West Indies, off the coast of Venezuela, where she was to take on fuel oil for delivery to Capetown, South Africa. Her recently installed three-inch World War I vintage guns sat on her bow and stern. She was manned by a regular crew of 41, plus 6 U.S. Navy guardsmen from the newly formed Armed Guard.

In her engine room Willard Hesse, an oiler, stood the 8 p.m. to midnight watch. Before going below to his duty station, he had stayed on deck in the warm, late afternoon sun as the ship rounded Florida's Cape Canaveral. The sight of the masts of a torpedoed ship jutting above the water gave him a scare. But the *Java Arrow* had passed safely, and as he oiled the engine's cross heads in the noisy, hot engine room, Willard felt a sense of calm for the first time since they had left New York harbor. He turned to Philip Shera at the engine controls, and shouted above the noise, "I think we're going to make it!"

Shera nodded his head as he adjusted a hand wheel.

The yacht *Kitsis*, a 30-foot, white cabin cruiser, moved at five knots, making a wide turn several miles to the south of Bethel Shoal. If she were down by the Fort Pierce Inlet, she might look like she was coming in late from a day of commercial fishing for dolphin in the Gulf Stream.

On the bow, Ottie Roach swept his eyes north, then south, looking not for submarines but for ship traffic running without lights. His fear was seeing the black silhouette of a large tanker bearing down on them.

This was the eighth night in a row that he and Kit Johnson had been offshore. Ottie felt tired. He glanced at Kit, the boat's owner, who stood at the helm, turning the wheel, a cigarette hanging from his lips. Ottie cupped his hands around his mouth and shouted, "Good night for tarpon fishing."

Kit removed the cigarette and hollered back, "That was last year."

The *Kitsis*'s instructions were to run a north-south, five-mile loop off Vero Beach. Their mission had never been specifically stated. Just get offshore with whatever other civilian boats the Coast Guard could scrape together and make the German submarines think U.S. Navy sub chasers covered the ocean. Of course, they had no machine guns, no depth charges — weren't even told what to do if they saw a sub. On board, Kit had a .22-caliber target pistol and a 12-gauge shotgun. In the four months they had been out on these patrols, Ottie and Kit had yet to see a torpedoed ship, much less a German submarine.

Chapter 2

Shell Point
1987

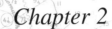

O N MAY 17, 1989, the Lufthansa L-1011 lifted off the runway at Miami International Airport. I heard the landing
gear clank into place as it folded into the fuselage. I was
flying across the Atlantic Ocean to Germany to meet a
famous war hero. After a two-year search I had located
Peter Cremer, the U-boat commander who had torpedoed the American tanker *Java Arrow*.

I peered out the window as the Orange Bowl, the skyscrapers of
downtown Miami, Biscayne Bay, and Miami Beach passed below,
while the jet climbed out over the city, eastward toward the ocean. I
could see the distinct edge of the Gulf Stream, dark blue against the
green coastal waters.

Two years earlier, on a hot summer day, my 80-year-old father, Kit
Johnson, and I sat on a bench by the water. His still strong hand
grasped mine in a grip I knew I would have to pry loose when I left.

We looked out on a man-made lagoon surrounded by neatly clipped lawns, condominiums, and the nursing pavilion of Shell Point Village, in Fort Myers.

A breeze rippled across the water from the Caloosahatchee River and Fort Myers to the east. A magnolia tree's leaves rustled over our heads. A tarpon rolled in the lagoon, breaking the black surface of the water, the fin and silver scales on its side sparkling for an instant in the sun.

"Look, Pappy," I said.

But he didn't see the fish, or no longer recognized it. And yet, he had caught a 125-pound tarpon on a fly rod, a great feat, particularly 20 years ago before fly-fishing had become so popular. He had treated the catch matter of factly, certainly didn't mount it, didn't even have a picture. But I knew it meant a lot because he would smile if I brought it up. He tended to disregard his accomplishments, and maybe I did, too.

Dad came from a family that expected a man to achieve some kind of stature in life, to be a business success, to have prestige in the community. Most of the rest of the men in the family had, particularly my Uncle Howard, Dad's twin brother, who had become president of the family business in West Virginia. My dad had left that business and moved to Florida in the 1930s, after having been told by a doctor that because of his ulcer condition, he had better take life easy. After World War II, Dad had started a sporting goods business, but it never really had panned out.

As I sat beside my father, I tried to make conversation. I talked about his one-year-old twin great-granddaughters, reminisced about the last time he and I had fished in the Florida Keys, told him about my work on a project in Miami. I ran out of words. We sat quietly, more comfortable with the silence than talking. That was the way it had always been whether we were riding in his jeep, running a boat, standing on the beach fishing, or drinking a beer in the back yard.

Dad broke the silence with a burst of gibberish, a noise-like static from a radio. I deciphered a word, "Sissie," and knew he was asking for my mother.

"Mom will be here in a few minutes."

He said nothing.

In our silence my right hand began to go numb in his grip. With my left hand I loosened his fingers, slipped my hand free and shook it to get the blood flowing again, letting him hold my other hand. A grunt came from his throat.

"What, Pappy?" I asked. He didn't respond. All I heard was the breeze blowing through the leaves over our head and the water in the lagoon rippling against the sea wall.

Sitting there linked to my father, I thought about the sketchy details of his World War II feats. He never made much of it. Wasn't most everyone a hero in the war? My Uncle Howard had received two medals for heroism as commanding officer of a minesweeper in the Mediterranean. But Dad had no medals. His war action had come before he even went into the Coast Guard; he had been a civilian, a volunteer, but every night he served on the front line of a sea war that was being lost, and not a lot of people knew about it.

I thought about his unseen adversaries, the German U-boat commanders who, in 1942, Hitler sent 4,000 miles across the Atlantic to attack ships in U.S. waters and who had involved people like my father in a war. Were all of these commanders heroes in their country? Had any of them survived the war? If so, they too would be old men.

Driving home that afternoon from Shell Point, across the state to Vero Beach, my mind was full of U-boats and tankers. I remembered that when I was 15, I had found, in a school library, Samuel Eliot Morrison's classic volumes about the U.S. Navy in World War II. Wondering if he had written about the German subs off Florida and the volunteer activities of people like my dad, I searched the books until I found a map indicating where the subs had attacked ships in Florida waters. Among the victims had been the SS *Amazone* and the USS *Java Arrow*. I knew those names: Dad had rescued the crew of the tanker *Java Arrow*; and for years, as I grew up, a name plate (or as it was called, a quarter board) from the freighter *Amazone* sat on the dresser in my room. But since then as I had attended college, got married, raised a family and pursued a career, I'd scarcely given thought to the U-boats or the war.

Several weeks after the Shell Point visit, in the midst of a family get-together at our home in Vero Beach, I talked my mother and my oldest son, Buck, into going with me the 15 miles to the county museum in Fort Pierce.

Buck wondered what I was looking for. He was at the wheel as we drove down U.S. 1.

"What kind of wild goose chase is this, Rody?" my mother chimed in. "I came with you all just to enjoy your company."

"I don't know," I replied, looking at Buck. "That's where the Coast Guard station is. That's where your grandfather kept the boat and where the survivors were brought in."

"Gramps told me the stories about the war, but I don't remember much about it," Buck acknowledged. As the oldest of our four children, he had been the closest to his grandfather, having the strongest interest in boats. Now a captain in the Army, tall, with a GI haircut, he hadn't seen his grandfather for several years, this man who had taught him to run a boat, to fish, and to love the water. Buck preferred to remember Gramps as he had been.

As we stopped for a red light to make the turn off U.S. 1 and head over the causeway to the museum, Mother spoke. "Rody, didn't you have something from one of the ships?" she asked.

I turned. She sat erect in the back seat wearing a blue-striped sport dress, a slight figure looking more like a young girl than a woman in her early 70s. Only the gray hair and the wrinkles in her face, tanned from the years shared with Dad in the outdoors, told her age. She had a cigarette in her mouth, which bothered me. The doctor had told her that she had emphysema and that her lungs were deteriorating.

I answered, "A name plate from the *Amazone*. I was just thinking about it."

"But Kit didn't rescue survivors from the *Amazone*," said Mom. "It was the *Java Arrow*. I don't remember anything about the *Amazone*."

"Mom, the name plate was the one I had on my dresser growing up. Dad got it somewhere. It disappeared when you all moved over to the beach."

"Yes, I remember it now. I wonder what happened to it?" She paused and took a drag on her cigarette. "I don't know why you're worrying about all this. It's over and done with. But if you persist, the person you should talk to is Ottie Roach."

"Who's Ottie Roach?" asked Buck.

"A friend of your grandfather's. They fished together when we first came to Florida. He was with Gramps when they rescued the crew from the *Java Arrow*," she replied.

I remembered Ottie. "Is he still alive?"

Mom pulled on the cigarette then flicked ashes out a crack in the window. "I think so, but I haven't seen him in years. Last I knew he worked for the fire department. Ottie could tell you all about the rescue, but he's probably diddle-headed like the rest of us."

"I'd like to see him," I said.

"Wasn't there something about Gramps running into some German subs?" asked Buck.

I nodded a "yes" and pointed to a faded sign that read "Saint Lucie County Museum." Buck pulled the car into an empty parking lot in front of a dilapidated building, a relic from the World War II naval amphibian base where troops had been trained for the June 6, 1944, D-Day invasion of Normandy. The museum sat on the edge of the Fort Pierce Inlet.

We entered the old building; it smelled like an attic. As our eyes adjusted from the bright sun outside, an elderly lady approached from an alcove and offered her help.

"We're trying to find anything that might be related to the tanker sinkings off the coast here during World War II," I said.

She didn't know much about that. "I didn't move here until the fifties, but you all look around. We have some interesting arrowheads and pottery from the Seminole Indians." She retreated to her desk.

"This isn't exactly the Smithsonian," commented Buck.

Long tables full of knickknacks filled a large room. The place looked more like a flea market than a museum. I rummaged around. Mom and Buck stood in a corner talking. On one table covered with an old sextant, a pair of dividers, and other marine artifacts, I came across an odd device. It looked like a pistol, but with a broad, stubby barrel. Then I recognized it — an old flare gun. Dad had kept one like it on the *Kitsis*.

It triggered a memory. One night, probably before the war, Dad had launched a flare out over the marshy muck pond by our house. As little as I was, I still knew it was unusual for my father to do something like that. He must have had a couple of his favorite bourbon and sodas.

"Won't somebody think a plane has crashed or something?" I asked, thinking that what he was doing was wrong but hoping he would shoot the flare anyway.

"Those flares have been sitting around too long. They need to be checked." He pulled the trigger and the flare rocketed into the dark sky. I watched fascinated as the red glow floated earthward on its small parachute.

I picked the gun off the museum table and looked at a white tag tied to the trigger guard. When I deciphered the smeared pencil writing, my heart pounded. I had to catch my breath before I could read aloud, almost yelling, "Flare gun from the tanker *Java Arrow!*"

Buck and Mom looked at me like I had lost my mind, then came over to see what I held in my hand.

"Do you have to be so noisy, Rody?" my mother cautioned.

"I wonder how they got this? Could it have been with the crew Dad rescued?" I asked.

"That's something! Maybe we ought to go look at the Coast Guard Station and see what they have," suggested Buck.

"We need to be thinking about getting home soon. I want to take a little rest before dinner," said Mom.

I laid the flare gun back down on the table almost not wanting to leave it.

As we drove alongside the inlet to the Coast Guard Station, we passed the Fort Pierce Yacht Club. Mom noted that this was where Dad had kept his boat. "I used to come down here and clean her up after they'd been offshore all night. The day after they rescued the tanker crew, it was God-awful — blood and vomit all over the deck and in the cabin. I didn't go back down there after that. It made me worry too much. The crew left some gray blankets that I brought home and washed. Rody, you took them to college. They still around?"

"We have 'em. They're in a box with our camping gear," I replied.

The Coast Guard Station wasn't the wooden two-story building with the red roof that I remembered, but a modern concrete-block structure. We entered and stood at a counter. Two immaculately uniformed young Coast Guardsmen sat monitoring a radio that crackled with the sound of yachtsmen and fishermen out on the water enjoying the weekend. We asked if the station had any World War II records. They didn't think so. When I mentioned that German U-boats had sunk ships in these waters, one commented, "Is that right?"

I felt disappointed. They didn't really care. I wanted them to go ask someone else about the records, but I knew it was no use.

Later, an envelope arrived from Mom with two folded newspaper pages, brown with age, clipped from an August 1945 *Miami Herald*. She had included a note, "Found these tucked away in your baby book."

The headlines read: "Nazis Sank 24 Ships Off Florida" and "State Men Had Brush With Subs." I couldn't believe it. I'd never seen these before. In a brief paragraph, the first article mentioned the *Java Arrow* and the fact that the crew had been rescued by Kit Johnson and Ottie Roach. The second short article told about a fishing boat running up on three German submarines. The article didn't mention my father's name or Ottie's, but it verified Dad's story.

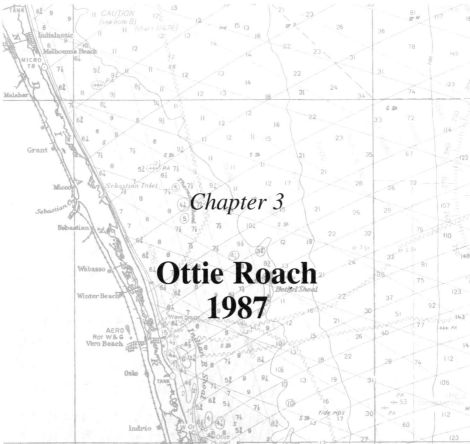

Chapter 3

Ottie Roach
1987

*T*HE JET leveled off at cruising altitude out over the Gulf Stream between Miami and Bimini, in the Bahamas. I started to settle back in my seat, but then decided to take one more look out the window. Far below, hardly bigger than a speck, a white fishing boat cut a wake across the blue-green water — probably a boat about the size of the *Kitsis*. Fifty years ago, before the war, it could have been Dad and Ottie Roach heading for the Bahamas for a week of fishing. I remembered a recent conversation with Ottie.

Ottie came in the back door, greeting me, "I brought you something." He handed me a brown envelope.

It was a couple of weeks after the trip to the museum in Fort Pierce, and I had called Ottie at my mother's suggestion. On the phone he remembered me instantly. I told him I was trying to find out something about Dad and the war, had some questions, and asked if he would come over to the house. He said sure and we set up a time. He said he hadn't seen my dad in a long time.

As he walked into the house, my memory of him remained as vivid as if I was still a child. In my mind he was still 30 years old: the lanky frame, perpetually tanned face, sandy hair, with a distinct Midwestern voice — not what you would expect from a fellow who had spent all his life in Vero Beach. He wore a sport shirt and khaki pants, just as I remembered he always had. Then I realized that he must be near 80.

I hadn't seen Ottie in years. With growth, Vero had lost the small town atmosphere where you saw everybody at least every once-in-awhile. While Dad and Ottie had been close fishing together in the '30s and during their volunteer patrols in the early stages of the war, they had drifted apart when Dad went into the Coast Guard. After the war Dad was involved in the Florida Sporting Goods store, and Ottie had an electronics repair business and later was an inspector for the fire department. They saw each other occasionally but then lost touch when Mom and Dad had sold their house west of town and had moved across the river to Riomar where Dad played golf every day.

I led Ottie through the living room and out onto the enclosed porch. The air conditioner whirred, fighting the muggy August heat. Ottie looked through the French doors at the patio, the oak trees, and the grassy sweep to the lake.

"Pretty place you got here."

"Yeah," I said. "Dad gave us the lot when we moved back to Vero."

"And that's Kit's place across the lake? I remember it."

"It was. It's where I grew up. Mom and Dad lived there twenty-five years. They moved to the beach about the time I finished college."

Ottie asked if Kit had developed the rest of the property.

I replied, "The lake was a muck pond. Dad convinced a local contractor to bring in a drag line, dig the lake, and take the muck for fertilizer. The contractor put in a shell road, and Dad sold the lots to people he liked."

"Well, it's mighty nice. I read in the paper that Kit found prehistoric animals or something like that in the lake?"

"The drag line kept digging up bones. Dad sent 'em off to the University of Florida. They weren't too impressed. Saber-toothed tigers and woolly mammoths roamed Florida ten thousand years ago and their bones turn up regularly. Look at this thing Dad had mounted." I pointed to a

Lucite block on the bookshelf encasing the molar of a woolly mammoth. "The Smithsonian doesn't have anything that nice."

"Kit did some interesting things," remarked Ottie. "That sporting goods business he had was really something. I wish he had kept that going. It's been a long time since I've seen him. How's he doing?"

"You know he has Alzheimer's."

Ottie nodded, squeezing his eyes shut for an instant.

"Physically he's in pretty good shape," I told him. "But he doesn't recognize anybody. Maybe knows Mom every once in a while. He has nurses; they take him out and walk with him every day. He's in a place on the water."

Seeing Ottie, this vital man still getting a boot out of life, made me miss my father. Tears welled up. Yet, he and Dad came from different backgrounds — Ottie, a second-generation Florida cracker; my father, coming to Vero Beach by way of Riomar, a wealthy winter colony. But they were alike in many ways. I could understand why they had been friends and fishing partners. They were quiet, practical men, competent with their hands, comfortable in the elements if not always elsewhere. These things I loved in my father and respected in other men of his generation.

"How's Sis doing?" Ottie asked.

"She's fine. Still raising cane. Keeps that place they live in jumping. It's run by a church and she calls it Jones Town. The church doesn't approve of smoking or drinking, but she walks around the place puffing on a cigarette and offers the minister a drink when he comes to call."

I asked Ottie if he ever saw the picture of Mom holding the turkey. He replied he hadn't.

"Well, in the sixties she and Dad took up bow and arrow hunting. I don't think he ever killed anything, but she did. In the picture she's in her hunting outfit with a little hat on her head holding this dead turkey by its feet, head down. An arrow is sticking straight out of its butt."

"She's a pistol!" Ottie added, "I never met a woman who hunted and fished with a man like she did with Kit. I guess it goes back to him being so sick when they first came down here.

"How long have you been in this house, Rody?"

"Twenty some years. I was working in Southern California and we decided to move back."

"You get ulcers like your dad? Kit said it ran in the family."

I replied that I had ulcers but they weren't bad.

"I brought you some pictures. Open that package." Ottie gestured to the envelope he had given me.

Sitting down on the couch, we spread faded brown photographs on a low table in front of us. He pointed, "Here's the *Kitsis*. We sure had some times on her."

I looked at the boat. She seemed smaller than I had remembered her as a child. Dad had named all his boats *Kitsis*. I always thought of it as a funny name; it rarely entered my head that it was the combination of my mom's and dad's first names. The photograph of the boat Ottie and I were looking at was *Kitsis III*, and I imagine the last boat Dad had was at least *Kitsis XII*. He finally gave up boats when his memory got so bad that he would forget where he was. My remembering his boats was like trying to recall the cars a person drove over a lifetime.

"So this is what you and Dad went to war with?" I asked.

"That's her."

"And you picked up a bunch of survivors in that?"

"Practically sunk her," Ottie declared.

We rummaged through the photographs. One showed Dad leaning back on the forward deck: no shirt, tanned, khaki pants, wind blowing through rumpled, curly hair already receding. His face showed cherub cheeks, the results of an all-milk diet, a remnant of his ulcer problems. He wouldn't eat baby food, so he drank milk. At one point he weighed 200 pounds, and at five-foot-eight was pretty chubby.

"I remember this." I peered at a picture of a whale shark hung head down from a crane, from a story in the *Miami Herald*. It looked like a gigantic black dewdrop tapering from its thin wisp of a tail to the huge head and mouth hanging open across its entire width. In miniature, one hand resting on the side of the monster's head, stood Kit Johnson. He wore a black full-length slicker and a white brim hat. Next to him was Ottie, his extended arm grasping the tip of the shark's side fin. Ottie was almost a head taller than Dad. They resembled Mutt and Jeff. Ottie's shirt hung out in front; he had a mate's hat perched on his head. Both looked exhausted, but their confident look indicated that they could do the same every day. The whale shark was 22 feet long and weighed over a ton.

"Dad told me you harpooned it."

"Yeah," Ottie said with just the slightest touch of a smile. "We ran up on it lying on the surface. Kit eased the *Kitsis* alongside, and I harpooned it in the side. That whale shark pulled us all over hell and back and into

the evening. When it finally wore out, we towed it into Fort Pierce, thinking we could sell the meat to the shark fishermen, but they weren't interested — didn't want anything that big. Kit had to pay someone to pull it
back offshore for the regular sharks to eat. Hell, a world-record marlin was
also caught off the *Kitsis*, too. You knew that."

I replied that it had been mounted in the bank downtown for years.

"It was a beauty," exclaimed Ottie.

"Didn't you all catch five sailfish off the *Kitsis* one day?"

"Yeah, that was the winter before the war. Howard, Kit's brother, was
with us. He was a competitive sort of guy. He and Kit had a contest over
who could catch the most sails that day. I was running the boat. Howard
won. Picked up a fish on the way in — and he had never fished much!"

I told him Howard had died of Alzheimer's a few years ago.

For some reason I kept putting off why I had invited Ottie out to talk.
Maybe I was afraid he wouldn't have any more to say about the war than
Dad did. I led into the conversation by asking him about the SS *Amazone*,
the freighter owned by the Royal Dutch Shipping Company, of Amsterdam, that had been sunk shortly after the *Java Arrow* had been torpedoed.

"Do you know anything about the quarter board from the *Amazone* that
Dad gave me? Did you all have anything to do with that ship?"

Ottie didn't recall a thing.

"Well, then tell me about you and Dad rescuing the crew of the *Java
Arrow*," I asked.

"I'll tell you what I can. I had a heart attack a few years back, and I
think it affected my memory."

Ottie settled back on the couch. I asked him if he wanted a beer, then he
began to talk.

Chapter 4

Kitsis
1942

OTTIE FLICKED OFF the light in the projection booth of the Florida Theater, climbed down the balcony stairs, and walked into the lobby. When the feature ended, he had rewound the film on another reel so it would be ready to run that evening. He had shown a movie starring Loretta Young, to a matinee crowd of 20 people scattered about the theater. As he passed through the lobby he glanced at a coming attraction poster for a Thursday double feature — admission 22 cents — walked by the concession stand, the ticket booth, and out the double swinging doors into a blinding late afternoon sun. Across the street the two-story Delmar Hotel cast a shadow across its front lawn. With the winter tourists gone, the place stood deserted.

Ottie had a half hour before Kit would pick him up to go down to Fort Pierce for the nightly patrol on the *Kitsis*. He stepped into McClure's Drug Store next door to the theater, thinking he might as well grab something to eat. No one except Emma was in the store. He slipped on to a stool next to the soda fountain. "Emma, give me a ham sandwich and a Coca Cola."

"Movie good?" she asked.

Ottie replied it was o.k. He wasn't thinking about the movie, but about the war news on the Movietone reel that had been shown before the feature — the Nazis bombing cities in England, MacArthur leaving the Philippines, the B-25s taking off from a carrier for the raid on Tokyo. Ottie wanted to be in the war, not just going offshore every night, and certainly not sitting around Vero Beach, showing movies to old people and school kids.

He guessed he was doing what he could, but still it wasn't like being in the service. Three months ago in February, a Coast Guard officer had come to Vero and organized a unit of the Coast Guard Auxiliary. Ottie and Kit and a bunch of other local men, who were too old for the service or were 4-F, had signed up. They had made Kit's friend, Press Gardner, flotilla commander. Ottie supposed that was because Press had the biggest boat in town, a slick, 50-foot Chris Craft.

Ottie had tried to enlist, but had been turned down because of a hernia. He had taken the train up to Jacksonville and then a bus out to Camp Blanding to try to get a waiver from the Army doctors. They said no. So he was 32 years old and labeled 4-F. He had watched almost every man in town either enlist or get drafted and here he sat. Of course, Kit hadn't gone. With his stomach condition he hadn't even tried. Ottie had trouble rationalizing how they were good enough to be submarine fodder, but not good enough to be accepted into the service.

The "ooga-ooga" from the horn on Kit's Model A sounded from the street. Ottie got off the stool, left 50 cents on the counter to cover the coke and sandwich, waved at Emma, and walked out the door. He crossed the street and slipped into the front seat of the car.

"How's the movie business?" asked Kit.

"Slow. Anybody going with us tonight?"

"Harry McDonald and Ward Lockwood. I ran into Harry at the hardware store and he said that he and Ward wanted to see what the war front was like. I told him it was damn dull. They're going to meet us at the boat."

Kit shifted the car into gear, and they headed down main street past the Five and Dime, the Indian River Citrus Bank, and Horace Gifford's filling station. Horace was shutting down his pumps. Kit stuck his head out the window and hollered at him, "Wanta go?"

Horace shook his head and shouted back, "Can't tonight." Horace was a hunting buddy of Kit's.

Ottie settled back in the seat for the 20-mile drive to the Coast Guard Station in Fort Pierce. Going out of town, they passed the cemetery and the converted boarding house that was the county's hospital, and rolled down the narrow strip of asphalt labeled U.S. 1, but which everybody called Old Dixie Highway.

Kit sat quietly, a hand on the wheel, puffing on a Camel and flipping the ashes out the window. Next to him lay his blue bottle of Amphojel. Every once in a while he would pick it up, unscrew the cap and take a long swig, leaving a white mark on his mouth which he wiped off with the back of his hand. He said it kept the gas down. He had drunk that stuff as long as Ottie had known him. Before Kit had moved to Florida from West Virginia, he had an operation to remove part of his stomach. Somebody had told Ottie that Kit had almost died from ulcers. That was why he had moved to Vero with his wife, Sis, and their little boy. Something about how he needed to take it easy, couldn't work anymore — would die otherwise.

Ottie had run into Kit at the city dock shortly after he had bought the *Kitsis*. Kit was always looking for someone to go fishing. And Ottie had the time when he worked the evening shows instead of the matinees. Now, it was just the reverse. He worked the matinees so he could go on the night patrols.

What Ottie liked about this short, stocky fellow sitting next to him was that Kit loved to fish, to be out on the water. They had had some times together, all right — harpooning the whale shark, the trip when Kit's brother, Howard, had visited and they caught all those sailfish.

"Has Howard gone in the service?" asked Ottie.

"Yeah, he just went in the Navy. Got a commission as a Lieutenant J.G. [*Junior Grade*] Lucky guy." Kit was looking straight ahead through the windshield as the Model A zipped along under the oak trees that overhung the road. He took another swig of the Amphojel.

Kit and Ottie drove directly to the Fort Pierce Coast Guard Station and checked in with the Lieutenant. They received instructions not to go out until 9:30 p.m. for reasons that weren't explained. Usually they were already offshore by dark. They were to patrol five miles off Vero until dawn. They drove over to the yacht club where the *Kitsis* was docked and boarded her.

The cruiser wasn't fancy like some of the yachts that the winter visitors had, but she did the job. She was 30 feet long, had a lapstrake hull, and

The *Kitsis*, a 30-foot cabin cruiser, figured prominently in the rescue of the USS *Java Arrow* crewmen by Kit Johnson and Ottie Roach.   *Ottie Roach*

looked like someone had mismatched the cabin with a skiff. The cabin extended low from the bow then rose abruptly to provide a protected area for the skipper at the wheel. Belowdecks, forward, were two bunks, the head, and a small galley with an ice box. A canopy stretched aft, but left an open cockpit for a couple of fighting chairs and plenty of room to hoist fish over the transom. She had a make-shift flying bridge, a metal rail, chair, and controls on top of the canopy. Outriggers mounted on either side of the cabin could be raised or lowered; but they had been removed for the patrols. A metal rail surrounded the bow. Kit had painted her white with green trim. Twin 90-horsepower marine engines pushed her along at eight knots.

Harry and Ward were already there. The four men sat around and talked for a couple of hours. Then Kit fired up the engines, Ottie and Ward cleared the lines, and Harry started the coffee. Kit eased her from the dock and headed out into the inlet. Someone waved at them, as they passed, from the top of the 50-foot Coast Guard observation tower on the south side of the inlet. Ottie noted the incoming tide, the buoys leaning shoreward, as they went out between the long rock jetties. The weather was good; a light breeze pushed two-foot seas from the southeast. From off-shore they could see the lights of Fort Pierce and Vero Beach glowing off the clouds. To the east, Ottie picked out the stars, but otherwise they were surrounded by a dark, rolling sea with flashes of phosphorus in the water. Kit sat in the pilot's chair steering the boat. Occasionally he'd pull the cloth off the compass to check the heading. The compass dial showed the only light on the boat except for the flicker of a cigarette cupped in Ward's hand as he stood on the bow.

Ottie stood by Kit, both peering ahead into the dark. Ottie broke the silence. "I sure as hell miss us not being able to be out here catching sail-fish. But I guess we're after bigger fish, so the Coast Guard says. I'll believe it when I see it."

"Yeah, I just like being out on the water, maybe not so much at night," replied Kit. He took a swig of Amphojel.

They continued up the coast. Just off Vero, Ottie pointed out the lights of the Beachland Hotel. Kit said, "I guess this is about as far north as they want us to go. I wonder how they decide where we patrol each night. Do you think they know something they don't tell us?"

"I don't think they know anything," answered Ottie.

Kit suggested they let Ward get some rest.

Ottie cupped his hands and hollered at Ward on the bow, "Get Harry up and you take a little snooze? Then we'll switch off. I'll take the bow."

"I'm already up. You guys want coffee?" asked Harry from inside the cabin.

Ward went below. Harry came up with the coffee and handed a mug to Kit and one to Ottie. Kit took a sip and made a face, "This stuff would take the hair off a brass monkey's balls." Kit turned to Harry. "Sit in one of the fighting chairs and be the stern lookout. No sleeping."

"Aye-Aye, Captain." Harry gave Kit a mock salute and moved to the stern. Kit smiled, reached for his Amphojel, twisted off the top and took another swig. Finishing his coffee, Ottie gave his mug to Ward to take below, climbed out of the cockpit and moved forward, gripping the hand rail. He stood on the top of the cabin, balancing on the balls of his feet as the slow-moving boat rolled gently with the sea.

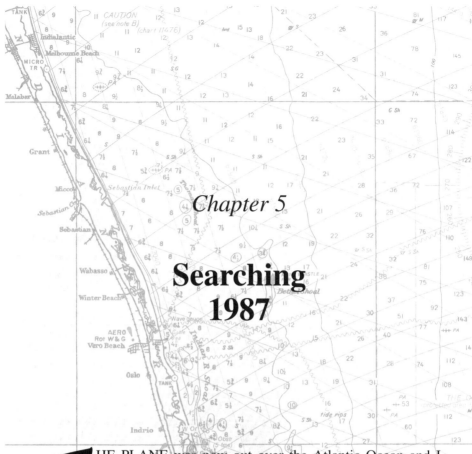

Chapter 5

Searching
1987

*T*HE PLANE was now out over the Atlantic Ocean and I figured it must be somewhere east of Bermuda. We had left behind what Peter Cremer had called "the fairway" during his Florida mission. On that "fairway" stretching from Cape Canaveral down the Florida peninsula, bordered on the east by the Bahamas and to the south by Cuba, the U-boats had torpedoed some 30 ships in six months mostly after dark.

I was drinking a beer, waiting for dinner. A blond woman next to me had been engrossed in a magazine since takeoff. I stretched, extending my legs as far as I could under the seat in front of me. I felt tired, but would I be able to sleep, to be fresh when I met Peter Cremer?

I had worked half a day and then driven four hours down I-95 to Miami to catch the flight. Daydreaming at the wheel, I almost missed the turn-off to the airport and would have continued on I-95 downtown. I had made that trip so many times from Vero to downtown Miami two summers earlier, to visit the Metro-Dade Library, where I had searched for information on the *Java Arrow* and German submarines.

During the summer of 1987, I had managed a project stringing fiber optic cable from one end of the city to the other connecting Metro Dade County's computer operations.

For years Miami had been a place to avoid. We, up the coast, perceived the city as a nightmare — rampant with traffic, riots, and drug lords. My dad hated cities, especially Miami. He would say, "Too many people pushing you around. I wouldn't go there on a bet." His only concession was to pass through on a boat going to the Bahamas or the Florida Keys. But he had been there off and on during the war.

After his exploits as a volunteer, the Coast Guard had forgotten about Dad's ulcers, took him in, and had him traveling all over the state for a while inspecting Coast Guard Auxiliary units. Mom traveled with him. They had never been apart, and they weren't going to let a war separate them.

Since I had to go to school, I stayed in Vero with my grandmother. The next year when Dad was running a patrol operation out of Tampa, they enrolled me in Florida Military Academy in Saint Petersburg. I was ten. But I saw Mom and Dad often, even riding on the Greyhound bus by myself on weekends to wherever they were. I remember staying with them in the Columbus Hotel in Miami with all the men in uniform.

On my return, after all these years, I was surprised to find I was enjoying the city; its cultural diversity, bustle, and tropical atmosphere gave it a foreign feeling.

Taking a breather downtown at lunchtime one day, I had wandered into the Metro-Dade Library. It was after Ottie had told me all about Dad's and his adventures on the *Kitsis*. As I roamed the stacks, I found the World War II section and forgot all about fiber optics and computers. I became a regular, climbing up the broad central steps of the building with its high windows to my soon familiar table and spent an hour after work searching before I began the drive back home to Vero Beach.

I found lots of information on U-boats as I scanned book indexes for the *Java Arrow* and the freighter *Amazone*. The *Java Arrow* popped up briefly a couple of times in one-line descriptions stating that it had been torpedoed and that it was unusual because it hadn't sunk. But I wasn't finding what I wanted. I hardly knew any more than when I had done my one-shot

research in the school library 40 years earlier. I wanted to see something
about the attack on the ship and the crew's rescue.

I kept looking until I had gone through every World War II book that
pertained to sea warfare. Discouraged and exasperated, I searched the
books on sunken ships, but all I found were on Spanish treasure ships sunk
along the Florida coast. I said to hell with the search. I had better things to
do. But I couldn't let loose. It was like fishing and it's time to go home,
but you keep making one last cast. I kept going back.

One day I looked at books in the general ship category. I came across
one that seemed out of place, entitled *A Careless Word . . . A Needless
Sinking*, that looked promising. Its cover showed a burning tanker and a
wounded, bedraggled crew rowing away in a lifeboat. I held my breath.
The book contained pictures of merchant ships and descriptions of their
sinkings. I leafed through the pages, fearing that the *Java Arrow* might not
be there. My heart leaped — I found it! A fuzzy photo of an old tanker
with an American flag on its side jumped out at me. Words tumbled from
the page. I wanted to yell to everyone in the library as I read "torpedoed
eight miles off Vero Beach" and saw words about a "powerboat from
shore" that participated in the rescue. I knew the powerboat had to be the
Kitsis, with Kit Johnson at the wheel. My father's action, if not his name,
was documented in history.

The description further stated that two of the crew had been killed in the
engine room during the attack. And there was a reference to the attacking
submarine and its commander: "*U-333* (Cremer)."

After I calmed down, I searched the book for a description of the *Amazone* sinking. I found nothing. But I did discover that the American tanker
USS *Halsey* had been sunk in the vicinity of the *Java Arrow* on the same
night by the same submarine. This fellow Cremer had been busy.

I hurried back up I-95 to Vero that evening, whipped into the garage,
and raced into the kitchen. "Guess what I found!" I shouted.

My wife, Katharine, looked up from the stove. I handed her the photo-
copy of the page with the picture of the ship and its description. She read
it.

"You found the *Java Arrow*!"

After dinner we were sitting at the table, just the two of us, and she
asked what I was going to do next.

"I'm not sure," I replied. "I want to know about, not just Dad, but about
a *Java Arrow* crewman, and the U-boat commander."

"Well," she noted, "you've got Dad covered with Ottie Roach, but what about the other two?"

"Don't know. I'll just keep searching. Wouldn't it be fun to find this guy Cremer?"

"What are the chances he survived the war?" she asked.

"Pretty slim. But according to the book, he wasn't the commander when the U-boat was sunk in 1944. Most of the German submarine crews were lost in action. And if he did survive, how would I find somebody in Germany?"

"If the U-boat commander survived, how old would he be?"

"Probably in his seventies, maybe a little younger than Dad," I guessed.

"If he lived through the war, he could still be alive," Katharine suggested.

I thought there was probably a better chance of finding someone off the *Java Arrow*.

Chapter 6

U.S. Merchant Marine 1988

*T*HE ARRIVAL by mail of the *Java Arrow* crew list from Captain Arthur Moore, the author of *A Careless Word...*, weeks after I had found his book in the Miami library, was quite a surprise. The handwritten list, titled "*Java Arrow* Survivors," had an attached note that read: "plus 2 lost, Chief Engineer and Third Assistant."

I had found Captain Moore through the Merchant Marine Academy at Kings Point, New York, after having called the director of the library, who informed me he knew Arthur Moore well. Moore lived on the Kennebunkport River up in Hallowell, Maine. He had graduated from the Academy and had sailed on merchant ships during World War II. He was a hero to the Merchant Marine for all the work he did on his book.

"You know," said the director, "he never found a publisher — had to pay for the printing himself."

I called Hallowell, Maine. In a gruff voice, Captain Moore told me that the *Java Arrow* was one of several hundred ships he had researched. He would have to hunt through his files to see what he could find, but wasn't sure he could identify any crew members.

The package Moore sent me included not only the crew list but an official Navy report, a photograph of the tanker, and a draft chapter possibly from a book of some sort. The Navy report had been the basis for the description of the attack and rescue in his book.

The photo showed the *Java Arrow* from the air, listing slightly to starboard with a hole in her port side at the waterline and an empty lifeboat lying alongside. It took another call to Captain Moore to find out about the draft chapter, which described the plight of one the engine room's crew, an oiler by the name of Willard Hesse. As Captain Moore recalled, he had received the document several years earlier from Mobil Oil, originally called Socony Vacuum Oil, the *Java Arrow*'s owner prior to the war. A college student, perhaps as a summer project for Mobil, had researched the company's wartime activity and may have written the chapter about the *Java Arrow*. Captain Moore suggested I contact the company directly to track down any of the crew.

All this information excited me. I was now optimistic about meeting a *Java Arrow* crewman. And I wanted a man who would remember being rescued that night by a small fishing boat —someone who would tell me about the brave volunteers who saved him. I called Mobil's New York headquarters and talked with someone in personnel who said he would compare the handwritten crew list that I had mailed to him against the retiree file.

After several more weeks, I received a call with two matches out of the 45 names on the list: Captain Jack J. Kelly, Jr., of Ventura, California, and Louis J. Festa of Piscataway, New Jersey. A check of the list showed that Kelly had held the rank of Able Bodied Seaman, a level comparable to corporal in the Army. Festa, as a Wiper, had been the equivalent of a private in the engine room crew.

My introductory letters to both men received no response, so after a couple of weeks I telephoned Jack J. Kelly. Mobil had told me that Kelly had been a tanker captain when he retired, and I felt that I had found the key to a personal account of the *Java Arrow* story. I dialed his home on impulse, without preparing a list of questions. Kelly's wife answered and summoned him to the phone. It took him a minute to recall my letter. He spoke politely in a strong voice but in a tone that conveyed, "Why are you bothering me?" He stated that he had never been on the *Java Arrow*. That threw me, and I didn't have presence of mind to explore the crew list with him. While I hesitated, he went on to say that he had been torpedoed three times — off Fort Lauderdale, Morehead City, North Carolina, and in the Gulf of Mexico. He added that he had retired after 44 years with the Mobil tanker fleet. The conversation ended right there, all in about 30 seconds. Kelly didn't say another word, and all I could do was say thank you and goodbye. I was discouraged. I had counted on this man.

There had been no telephone listing for Festa in Piscataway, New Jersey. I had given up on that one. The crew list appeared to be wrong, but I knew that the Captain's name, Hennichen, was correct. Was I ever going to get the story from a *Java Arrow* crewman's perspective? And to think that I might ever find the German submarine commander was really a pipe dream.

A couple of weeks later I received a call.

"Mr. Johnson, my name is Jim Festa. You wrote my father about the war," said a voice with a strong New Jersey accent.

"Yes, Jim. I appreciate you calling." I held my breath. Was this going to be the breakthrough?

"My father read your letter, but doesn't want to talk to you."

"Oh." I was disappointed.

"He had never talked about his wartime experiences until your letter came. Then he told me he had been sunk three times."

"I guess I can understand why he doesn't want to talk." I thought about Kelly. Was this the same situation? "Was your father on the *Java Arrow*?" I asked.

"Yes. He said he stayed in the water three or four hours before a destroyer picked him up. He told me the guy you sent the picture of looked familiar."

The picture showed my father in a Coast Guard uniform. The story of Festa's rescue wasn't the one that involved the *Kitsis*. Obviously, he had gotten his sinkings mixed up. I asked Jim, "How old is your father?"

"He's seventy-five. He does volunteer work at the hospital. He spent forty-five years in the Merchant Marine. He used to attend the Mobil Oil reunions but got bored with it."

"Jim, if I came up there, would he see me?" I asked.

"No. He would be mad if he knew I was calling you. He's kept your letter, but he says it was too long ago. And he says he doesn't give a damn about your interest in tracking down the German submarine commander who sank him."

"Were you a child during the war?" I asked, desperately trying to keep the conversation going and fearing that if it ended I would have nothing.

"Yes, we lived in Charlotte then; I remember my dad coming and going. I'm fifty-three. I'm divorced, I've lived with my father since my mother died."

I asked Jim if he would give me his telephone number.

"My business keeps me on the road so I'm hard to reach. It wouldn't be good to call the house with my dad there," he answered.

"Can I send you some information on the *Java Arrow* in case your father changes his mind?" I asked.

Jim replied that would be fine, and I thanked him for calling. I felt a tie to this man. We had similar concerns — fathers in old age who we were worried about, and fathers who might have been on the same small boat together, yet didn't know it. I wanted to talk to Jim Festa's father. I sent more information to Jim, hoping to trigger something, but never got a response. My hope for talking with a *Java Arrow* survivor was all but lost.

The story of the *Java Arrow* and her crew, as I had discovered, seemed to lay buried by the years in the misplaced archives of Mobil Oil, in the murky history of defunct shipping companies, in the lost personnel records of maritime unions, and maybe in the minds of the two living crewmen who did not want to remember — all of which were inaccessible.

So, I tried another approach. I visited the Mariner's Museum in Newport News, Virginia. Katharine and I stopped on our way to visit our youngest son, Charles, at his boarding school in Virginia. We spent all day flipping through marine journals and documents.

We discovered that the *Java Arrow* had led an adventurous life traveling the world's seas. Built in Quincy, Massachusetts, she had joined a dozen other "Arrow" Class tankers constructed by Socony Vacuum Oil, immediately after World War I, to assemble an ocean-going tanker fleet of some 40 ships. The design was based on the case oil trade for China. Apparently, the Chinese used oil from five-gallon cans to light the lanterns in their homes. The tankers, in addition to their 100,000-barrel bulk oil tanks, had a special dry-freight deck to carry these cans. However, by 1930, terminals at Far Eastern ports had built bulk storage tanks, and it was no longer necessary to haul the cans from the U.S. During the worldwide depression in the 1930s, the *Java Arrow* was shifted from the China trade to hauling oil from Texas to New York.

Also in the museum, Katharine and I found a beautifully built, five-foot model of an "Arrow"-type tanker that looked almost exactly like the photos we had seen of the *Java Arrow*. Studying the model and a drawing that we discovered in some files, we found that she was 460 feet long and 60 feet wide. We tried to relate these dimensions to something we knew other than small fishing boats: it was about the length of one and a half football fields.

The ship carried a 45-man crew, which seemed small for her size. Her forward deck house, narrow but three stories high, held the bridge, the captain's and officers' quarters, and the dining saloon. The rest of the crew lived two to a compartment in the aft deck house, which also contained the crew's mess and the ship's hospital.

On the drawing, we found the engine room, which lay below the water line toward the stern. A 3,000-horsepower steam engine, which had driven a propeller at least twice the height of a man, had moved the ship at ten knots. The smokestack stood just forward of the aft deck house. I showed Katharine where the two torpedoes had hit, one midships and the other right at the stern, as stated in the Naval report. That second torpedo was the one that had killed the two crewmen in the engine room.

We found enough *Java Arrow* history, in fact, to piece together her fateful voyage down the East Coast. After being torpedoed, she had been towed to Fort Lauderdale, the hole on her starboard side repaired, and towed back to Baltimore where a shipyard replaced her steam engine with a diesel. She went back to war and ended up hauling oil in the South Pacific. Afterwards, she had several different owners and was renamed *Kerry Patch*. In the museum's photo file, we found a picture of her in the '50s, looking old and tired, when as the *Celtic* she carried grain.

Some months later, I got a call from a doctor friend of mine who suggested that I talk to the husband of one of his patients. The man had been in the Merchant Marine during World War II, and was a "neat old guy."

Philip Neal and his wife lived in Barefoot Bay, on the Indian River, halfway between Vero Beach and Melbourne, a place with acres and acres of manufactured homes with well-kept lawns surrounding a couple of golf courses. Neal greeted me in a brown khaki shirt and khaki pants held up by wide red suspenders. He had a broad, friendly face, with wispy hair standing up on his head. I quickly found out that he had been the former Marine Superintendent at Mobil Oil and had been in charge of Mobil's tanker fleet until he had retired in 1984, with over 40 years in the company. And he had been with the company when it was called Socony Vacuum Oil. I asked him if he knew the *Java Arrow*.

"I know her. She was torpedoed during the war," he replied.

I then told him about my dad's rescue of the crew. "Would you have known any of the crew on her?" I asked.

"Oh," he hesitated, "I don't know. That was a long time ago."

I asked if he would take a look at the crew list Captain Moore had given me. He picked up his bifocals and scanned the list for a minute.

"Some of these names are familiar, men who stayed on at Mobil like I did, and sailed in the tanker fleet after the war," he responded.

"Did you know Jack Kelly or Louis Festa? I contacted them, but they didn't want to talk."

"Is that right? I don't understand why. I knew both of 'em. Kelly was a tanker Captain. I think Festa rose to Chief Engineer. I'm surprised he was only a Wiper back then."

Neal remembered, "That fellow Jack Kelly was something, a mischievous Irishman, the kind that would steal the cook's pies. When he was a Third Mate he had a BB gun and while his ship was going through the Panama Canal, he took pot shots through the porthole of his cabin at spectators. I sailed with him. He shot me in the butt once, and I threw the damn gun overboard."

"Now Louis Festa was comical," he continued. "He had back trouble and wore a corset. He wouldn't wear a shirt so the damn thing was always dirty."

Neal went on to describe the *Java Arrow* Master, Sigvird Hennichen, as "typical Scandinavian — aloof." Hennichen had been a career Captain with Socony Vacuum, and probably in his 50s, when the *Java Arrow* had been attacked. Neal told a story about how at sea Hennichen would have all his mates shoot the latitude with the sextant to calculate the ship's location, but the only one he entered in the log was the one he shot himself.

Philip Neal wasn't the only former Merchant Marine seaman that I ran across. I had read a book review in the *Miami Herald* by Frank Farrar, about his life in the Merchant Marine and his experiences on Liberty ships during World War II. He lived close by in a trailer park near the beach in Melbourne, across the river from where I worked. A tall, thin, enthusiastic fellow in his 70s, Frank told me about sailing down the Florida coast in 1944 and seeing the masts of sunken ships jutting out of the water around Cape Canaveral. I hoped he would be able to tell me what it had been like to be torpedoed at night and have to abandon ship. But he couldn't fill in that part of the story. He had been at Normandy, in the Mediterranean, and had steamed across the Atlantic in convoys several times, but he had been lucky enough never to experience a sinking.

I may not have found *Java Arrow* crewmen who would talk, but I did discover a ship that gave me a feel for the tanker. On a trip to San Francisco to visit my son Buck, an Army Captain stationed at Fort Ord, we saw a sign at Fisherman's Wharf that read, "See the *SS Jeremiah O'Brien,* America's last Liberty Ship." Liberty ships had been mass produced during the war to haul supplies across the Atlantic to Europe and to the Pacific theater.

I asked Buck, "Do you want to go?" He said sure. I buttoned my sport coat against the chilly breeze coming off the bay, and we started hiking. We walked through Fort Mason, came over a rise, and saw this huge freighter laying alongside a pier. Beyond stood the Golden Gate Bridge.

The *O'Brien*'s shape didn't look anything like the pictures of the *Java Arrow*. But as we mounted the gangplank and toured her, I learned that there were many similarities between the two ships.

In two hours, Buck and I explored every nook and cranny of the *O'Brien,* scampering about like kids, hollering, "Come look at this!" as we discovered the maze of decks, cabins, hallways, and ladders. "Isn't this neat?" Buck marvelled.

The size amazed me. It seemed that 50 men manning the ship would have been lost in its vastness — quite a contrast to 50 men packed in a U-boat. I examined the guns, particularly the three-incher on the bow, which must have been like the gun mounted on the *Java Arrow*.

The *O'Brien* looked immaculate; everything had been freshly painted. Someone took exquisite care of this ship. We noticed older men throughout and discovered that they belonged to a group of retired Merchant Mariners who cared for her. We talked with several of them. As an artillery officer, Buck wanted to know about the guns we had seen on the bow and the stern. The men were like Philip Neal and Frank Farrar; they seemed to fit a mold.

As we walked down the gangplank, leaving the ship, Buck commented, "They remind me of Gramps." I knew what he meant. I could see my father as one of them — unpretentious, practical, tied to the sea.

The last thing we had discovered on the *O'Brien* was its engine room. I opened a bulkhead door, stepped onto a platform, and I peered down into a cavern of black machinery, with only a row of bare lightbulbs penetrating the darkness. I smelled oil. I grabbed the cold handrail and step-by-step descended. Tanks, tubes, rods, shafts, pipes, gears, wheels, and cylinders rose all around me. The quietness of this place scared me, but I imagined it could be a real hell-hole with the noise of the machinery cranking and the heat generated by the engines. Forward, the two boilers rose into the darkness. To the rear, a shaft extended out of the central mass down a tunnel to the stern and connected to the huge propeller. At the engineer's station, a mouth tube ran upward to the bridge providing the only human link to the outside world. Here, 30 feet below the water line, the engine room crew worked in the noise and shadows and saw no sea or sky. I now knew what an engine room was like — the place where Shera and Fentress had been killed when *U-333* torpedoed the *Java Arrow*.

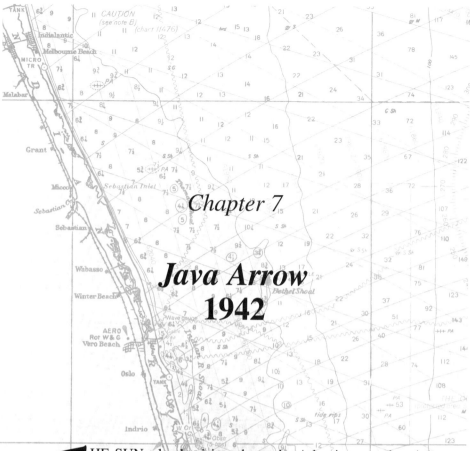

Chapter 7

Java Arrow
1942

THE SUN, slowly rising above the Atlantic, spread a pink glow over the Statue of Liberty and the top of the Empire State Building up the bay. Amidships on the *Java Arrow*, Willard Hesse leaned on the rail, squinted at the sun, gazed at the New York skyline, and then turned back to watch the tug push the tanker out into the Upper Bay from Socony Vacuum's New Jersey refinery docks at Bayonne. In a few minutes he would head below to the engine room for his watch as an oiler. He had pulled the eight to noon and the eight to midnight watches. Maritime Union rules dictated four hours on, eight hours off.

The tanker sat low, loaded with seawater ballast in her cargo tanks and drums of lube oil and ethyl fluid on the dry freight deck. She was dressed for war, with a gray paint job and gun emplacements on the bow and stern. When Willard had sailed on her six months earlier, she had no guns. She had displayed the Socony "S" on her smokestack and a gigantic American flag painted on her hull, just below her forward deck house. Prior to Pearl Harbor, the flag had identified her as neutral. But that had made no difference, for another Socony

The USS *Java Arrow*, with the Socony Vacuum Oil "S" on her stack. The American flag painted on her bow identified the tanker as a neutral in October 1941. *The Mariners Museum, Newport News, VA*

tanker had been torpedoed, with all hands lost in the mid-Atlantic, five days before the attack on December 7, 1941. Willard knew a couple of the crew who had been aboard.

The *Java Arrow* moved out into the bay, pushed along by the tug. As Willard sucked in the cool air of the early April morning and smelled the familiar mixture of salt water, rust, and oil, he thought about Mary's Grill, that dingy restaurant in Jersey City, where a couple of nights ago he and some of the crew had been drinking beer and eating hamburgers. The place had long, stained wooden tables with attached benches. A bar and stools stretched down one wall. From behind the bar, Mary — a large woman in a gray tent-like dress — supervised. Hamburger and onion smells floated out into the room from the swinging door to the kitchen. A Pabst Blue Ribbon sign blinked over the door to the men's room. The men sat at two of the side-by-side tables with elbows on the rough wood and mugs of beer in their hands. Tom Sweeney and Ted Crawford, two of the mates, were doing most of the talking.

"I wonder if we're going to have to hug the God-damn coast this trip," remarked Crawford. "They say the German subs are lying out there looking at New York. They're off Delaware, off the Chesapeake, off Hatteras. Even sitting on the beach in Florida."

"That's the rumor," replied Sweeney.

Willard, holding on to a beer, sat at the end of the table and listened uncomfortably.

Crawford pounded his fist on the table. "We don't have a chance! What are the frigging Navy and Coast Guard doing to protect us? I'll take my chances on the open sea. Odds got to be better for a sub not finding us out there. To hell with the Navy."

Sweeney put down his beer. "We got that three-incher on the stern."

"Yeah, that World War I barrel will probably blow up the first time it's fired. And that Navy gunnery crew, they don't act like they've ever seen a ship before."

"It's better than nothing."

"I don't know about that. All the Navy can say is 'Follow the ten-fathom curve and when you're torpedoed turn west and beach your vessel.' That's real encouraging."

Sweeney shook his head. "God-damn it, Ted, shut up. We do what they tell us. We shouldn't be talking in here. We need to get back to the ship. Let's go."

Following Sweeney's lead, Willard and the group stood up, each paid his bill, and left. Mary hollered,"Good luck, boys," as they trooped out the door into the cool night. Her words kept ringing through his mind.

Heading to sea gave Willard the same sense as waiting for the buzzer at the start of a high school basketball game. But this time there was a fear, a tingle of uneasiness that he had never experienced before. It was crazy to go out there with all those subs and no protection. The money was good — $100 a month plus some overtime, union wages, better than the GIs' — but was it worth risking his life? Though had he not been on this ship, he would have been drafted and probably fighting the Japs in some island jungle.

Willard looked up at the wing of the bridge and saw the Captain, Sigvird Hennichen, scanning the busy harbor traffic, probably looking for the Navy escort. Willard wondered if the Captain felt like he did; he hoped not. Hennichen was intimidating at times, but the older guys considered him a good man; he had been with Socony Vacuum for years. Willard figured if he was going on a suicide cruise it might as well be with Hennichen as anybody.

The *Java Arrow* moved slowly through The Narrows, between Staten Island and Long Island, through the open submarine net, out past the Ambrose Light Ship, and turned south around Sandy Hook Spit on which Fort Hancock stood, guarding the approaches to New York Harbor. The tanker had become part of a three-ship convoy with a World War I four-stacker destroyer leading the way.

At a meeting of the engine room gang in the crew's mess just before they had sailed, Chief Engineer Fentress announced their destination. "The Captain says it's Capetown, South Africa."

"Capetown! Let's go around the world. Give the Krauts plenty of opportunity to sink us," griped Paul Reese, one of the engine-room fireman.

Fentress told the men to "pipe down," and continued, "Our route goes down the East Coast past Florida to Cuba, through the Windward Passage, and across the Caribbean to Curaçao."

"If we get that far," one of the wipers grumbled under his breath.

If Fentress heard the comment, he ignored it. "We'll take on oil at the refinery at Curaçao and haul across the South Atlantic."

"Will we be in a convoy?" asked Willard.

"That's the plan."

"What about subs? Where are they?" asked Philip Shera, the Third Assistant Engineer.

"Nobody is saying, but the rumor is that a sub shelled a freighter off here the other night. There's problems around Hatteras, but the Navy says they'll escort us past there in daylight. OK, let's get the watch below."

That night Willard stood watch as the *Java Arrow* rested in the Harbor of Refuge at Lewes, Delaware. After passing Cape May at dark, she had arrived at this haven on the south side of Delaware Bay. When Willard got off watch at midnight, he grabbed some biscuits in the mess, went to his berth in the aft deck house, and slept.

At daybreak, the tanker weighed anchor and churned up the bay towards Philadelphia. Coming up on deck from the morning watch, Willard was surprised to see nothing but farm land. He suddenly realized that the ship was passing through the 100-year-old Delaware-Chesapeake Canal, cruising more like a slow-moving freight train than a great ocean-going vessel.

By nightfall, the *Java Arrow* had moved out of the canal and into the Chesapeake Bay. On duty that night, Willard felt better. With two days of survival behind and two days and 200 miles of inland water ahead, maybe the Navy was going to take care of them. On the other hand, the rumors kept flying through his head. In the four months since the war had started, the word was that Socony had lost several tankers and over a hundred men. He had some friends on other ships that he had been unable to track down, and when he had asked about them at the Maritime Union hiring hall, the only answer he got was that they didn't know.

The *Java Arrow* cruised down the Chesapeake uneventfully and on Thursday, April 30, entered the anchorage at Lynnhaven Roads near Virginia Beach. Again, Willard stood watch in a quiet harbor. The next morning, the tanker steamed out to sea as part of a seven-ship convoy headed around Hatteras.

Willard came off duty at noon and tried to sleep. Cape Hatteras was U-boat heaven. He had heard so many rumors of ships sunk in these waters — the German subs were just lined up, waiting for the kill. Finally, he got up and spent the late afternoon on deck despite the discomfort of a brisk northeast wind and swells that gave the ship a slight roll. Even if the risk was less in daytime, he wanted to be ready to abandon ship if a torpedo struck.

Leading a charmed life, the *Java Arrow* anchored safely that night at Cape Lookout, North Carolina, in a protective pen surrounded by a submarine net and mines. Willard felt a sense of relief. Somebody aft was playing a guitar. Jack Kelly, one of the AB's [*Able Bodied Seaman*], had his BB gun out, shooting at buoys. Maybe the worst was over. They had survived the run past Cape Hatteras. Perhaps the Navy did know what they were doing. There were no stories about Socony ships having been attacked in Florida waters or in the Caribbean.

Now traveling night and day, the small convoy sailed on down the coast past Charleston and Savannah. Willard noted that the *Java Arrow*, plodding along at ten knots, kept dropping farther behind the convoy. He could see that they finally had the sea to themselves. Philip Shera said that he had heard that the Captain was tired of the constant haranguing from the convoy commander in his patrol boat, who kept radioing the *Java Arrow* that the convoy wasn't going to slow for one laggard. Hennichen had said, "Let 'em go."

On Tuesday, May 5, the *Java Arrow*'s eighth day at sea, she passed down the Florida coast past Jacksonville, Daytona Beach, and around Cape Canaveral.

That night Willard was on his usual eight-to-midnight watch as the *Java Arrow* moved south of the Cape, hugging the coast. All was normal in the engine room. At 11:30 p.m., Willard saw Ted Peace, the fireman, go forward to call the next watch. Shera, the senior man in the engine room, took over Peace's duty.

Chapter 8

Peter Cremer
1989

*T*HE STEWARDESS placed my dinner tray on the drop-down table as I picked up my nearly empty beer to move it out of her way. With her other hand, she put down the tray for my seat mate, who still had her nose in a magazine. I was busy with thoughts of the *Kitsis*, the *Java Arrow*, and *U-333* so we hadn't talked.

As I picked up my fork, she slid her magazine into the seat pocket and, turning toward me, asked, "Are you going to Germany on business?"

"No, I'm on my way to see a man near Hamburg who brought his U-boat to Florida in 1942 to sink American ships. My father rescued the crew of one the ships he torpedoed."

"How fascinating. What is the U-boat commander's name?"

"Peter Cremer," I replied.

"The name sounds familiar. I am from Frankfurt. And how did you find this Peter Cremer?"

"It's a crazy story," I said.

She acknowledged she would be interested in hearing it,

I hesitated for a minute. There were certain things I didn't need to tell her. I would have sounded idiotic.

Initially absorbed in my search for *Java Arrow* information, I hadn't paid much attention to the U-boat commander who had torpedoed her, though he was always in the back of my mind. With my research on the tanker complete, this fellow Cremer began to obsess me, and I wasn't sure why. Yes, I needed information from the submariner's point of view, but there was more to it than that. I was searching for a hero in this story, and my father didn't seem to fit the mold. It was something I couldn't quite put my finger on as yet. And while I admired the Frank Farrars and the Philip Neals of the Merchant Marine, they were, in a way, too much like Dad. If, in my quest, I was indeed looking for a hero, then my last chance seemed to be Cremer. It didn't seem to matter to me that he was a German, that he had fought for Hitler. I wiped those kind of thoughts from my mind. The war had been over for years. When I had taken a vacation trip to Germany a few years earlier, I hadn't thought of the German people as enemies. Anyway, what I was looking for was a man who was close to the sea and who had been involved in heroic actions.

In the beginning, I could only develop this man in my imagination. I day-dreamed about him coming to Vero Beach to revisit the site of his war success, like the old soldiers who return to Normandy. In fact, I got so caught up in all this that I stared at men in their late 70s in airports on business travel or wherever, seeking a model for what the older Cremer might look like.

Pursuing my game, I had embarrassed Katharine on one occasion. We were sitting in a restaurant in Vero across the way from an older man with snow-white hair and his attractive wife. They spoke with an accent; it sounded like German to me. I stared with fascination during dinner. Had I found the model for Peter Cremer? I paid our bill, then totally out of character, walked over to his table and asked, "Excuse me, are you German?"

The distinguished-looking man put down his fork and replied, "No, we are from Denmark."

I felt like a fool. What was I doing? I fumbled through an explanation as to why I had asked which made things worse. Katharine stood behind me, wondering if her husband had lost his mind.

"No, I am not a submarine commander. We Danes don't particularly like the Germans," he remarked. Fortunately, he looked at me with amusement — another crazy American. Katharine had dragged me away.

My obsession with Cremer pestered me — this man about whom I knew nothing at the time, whether he was alive or dead. I even fantasized his return to the site of his first command:

> An elderly, foreign gentleman, well-dressed, enters the Ocean Grill, sits down and talks to the bartender. He says he is visiting Florida from Germany and that he had been the Captain of a submarine that had been off Vero Beach during World War II.
>
> The Ocean Grill, Vero's oldest and best-known restaurant, is perched on pilings on the edge of the beach, and at high tide the surf rolls in and out under its flooring. Sitting at the bar gives the feeling of being at sea. Someone sipping a beer there on the evening of May 5, 1942, might have not been so comfortable if he had known that U-boats lay off the beach and that shortly a tanker would be torpedoed in the vicinity. In fact, the back of the current Ocean Grill menu reads: "If you can believe the war stories during that time, the Nazis were sinking tankers offshore in front of the Grill."
>
> In my fantasy, the bartender knows Ottie Roach, knows that somehow he had been involved with German submarines during the war. The bartender calls Ottie and tells him he ought to come over and meet this guy. Ottie isn't sure he wants to do that, so he calls me. I get right back to the bartender and ask him to tell the German that I am coming right over.
>
> I walk into the Ocean Grill about five, well before the dinner crowd; only a few people are at the bar. Most look like tourists, but I figure the one sitting off to himself gazing out at the ocean is the right man. I introduce myself. He stands and shakes my hand. He is thin, gray-haired, an impressive elderly man. Speaking English clearly but with a distinct accent, he says his name is Cremer. He holds a gin and tonic. We sit down, and I order a draft from the bartender who I thank for calling.
>
> The German speaks easily but formally. He has flown into Miami on Lufthansa, rented a car, and driven up the coast. His

purpose is to return to Florida and see it firsthand, this time from the shore rather than through a periscope. A couple of nights earlier he had gone offshore out of Fort Pierce on one of those reef fishing boats that charge so much a head. He didn't fish, just relived a night off the Florida coast.

I tell him about the *Kitsis* and my father. Yes, he had torpedoed the *Java Arrow* and sunk another ship, the *Halsey*, the same night. I ask him to join me for dinner and to continue our conversation. He accepts and we are led to a table. He walks with a limp which I attribute to a war injury. We talk into the evening.

With time, realities replaced fantasies. I could tell this woman sitting next to me on this transatlantic flight some of the realities.

I took a sip of wine, which had replaced the beer; between mouthfuls of my dinner I began to talk.

"A couple of years ago I found information in a book that linked Cremer to the tanker he torpedoed and whose crew my father rescued. A few months later, I came across another book in a library about the exploits of several German submarine commanders. I flipped through the pages, didn't expect anything, just another one of the many books written about U-boats. Then I saw the name Peter Cremer. I almost died. There were all sorts of stories about him that portrayed him as a dashing guy who knew how to have a big time."

"What do you mean?" she asked.

"The author described Cremer something like 'blond with very light gray eyes, of medium build. Incapable of inactivity, in love with life.' And there was one story about his talking Admiral Doenitz into giving him money to go on a wild trip to Paris."

"It sounds like he was what you call a party-boy. Was there anything about his attack on the ship your father was involved with?"

"No. That was disappointing. But there was a story about him after the war, getting in touch with a British officer whose destroyer he had battled off Africa. At least that told me he had survived the war — a pretty rare feat for U-boat commanders. So there was a chance he could still be alive. And I wanted to know what he had done after the war, and what kind of man he was. I was really obsessed to find him, but didn't know how."

She asked what I had done to find Cremer.

I replied, "Very little. The most I could think of was to inquire of a few people I knew who had connections in Germany. Nothing came of that." I had had no luck talking with the *Java Arrow* crewmen, and now Cremer didn't seem like a possibility either.

I continued. "Six months passed, and I had all but given up the whole endeavor. Then one day on one of my visits to my dad, I stopped at a bookstore near the nursing home where he lives. I bought a book about German submarines. As I walked out the door, I glanced at the back flyleaf. Several related books were listed. I saw: *U-boat Commander*, by Peter Cremer. I screamed, 'Peter Cremer!' The bookstore owner thought I was crazy. I ordered the book, received it in three days, and read it in one sitting. There was a whole chapter on Cremer's Florida mission."

"That's exciting!" she agreed.

"The book gave me just a clue about his life after the war. The flyleaf said he lived in Hamburg and was a general manager for Sperry Electronics, an American company, of all things. The book had been published in 1984 so the chances that Peter Cremer was still alive seemed good. The book was great, but I still wasn't satisfied. Details about his life other than during the war were nil. And the book with emphasis on his war exploits told little about what kind of man he was. I still had to find Peter Cremer, and the book gave me a means to do it."

There was something else I had found out, but figured I was already overdoing it with this woman and didn't want to bore her any further, though she seemed fascinated with my tales. Cremer, on the same night that he had attacked the *Java Arrow* and the *Halsey*, also sank the *Amazone*, the freighter whose name plate I had once owned. I was excited about linking Cremer to the *Amazone*, that all these things happened on the same night. And it started me wondering again how my father had gotten hold of the *Amazone* name plate. I had no idea and no one to ask. Ottie had said he didn't know. Cremer's book also stated that the *Amazone* was Dutch. At least, that explained why she had not been included with the other two ships in Captain Moore's book, which covered only the U.S. Merchant Marine.

At this point, I figured I had talked enough so I asked my seat mate a question. "Was your father in the war?"

The SS *Amazone*, a freighter owned by the Royal Dutch Shipping Company, of Amsterdam, was sunk by *U-333* on the same night as the tankers USS *Java Arrow* and USS *Halsey*.

The Mariners Museum, Newport News, Virginia

"Yes, he fought on the Russian front. He was not a Nazi. My parents were not political," she replied.

She went on to tell me that she had been raised in postwar Germany with food shortages and amid ruins. Her schooling had reflected little about Germany's part in World War II. Hitler was hardly mentioned in her books. As a child, she had seen a documentary on the concentration camps, but there had been little explanation. Older people did not want to discuss the war, the young felt curiosity, anger, and shame about their country's involvement, and at times even resented their parents. Talking with her, I sensed I was being prepared for something I might run into in the future as I delved into the German past. How could these people, who today seemed so pleasant, fight for such a reprehensible cause? But, of course, they felt they had no choice. After all, we had people fight in Vietnam who felt the same way, and they weren't fighting for a Hitler.

She sat quietly for a moment, then broke my train of thought. "You still haven't told me how you found this U-boat commander."

I told her about contacting Cremer's American publisher, who referred me to his British publisher. I made a predawn call to London and chatted with an English lady who remembered the book and indicated it had been printed in several languages, but could not give me his address —"must protect the author's privacy, you know." She did suggest I write a letter to him in care of her company, and she would forward it. If he wanted to get back in touch with me, that was his choice.

An international call to England at one time would have seemed a major event, one that would have made me nervous. But after the Miami job, I had been assigned a project at work to provide air base communications equipment to Saudi Arabia through a Korean and Dutch consortium — my first exposure to international business — and overseas calls became daily happenings. I had stepped into the middle of this project and found myself facing irate customers, who threatened to cancel the job for lack of progress. I had had to make a trip to Amsterdam to deal with the problem.

With this new exposure to the foreign scene, finding a Peter Cremer in Germany no longer seemed quite so insurmountable.

By this time, the woman and I were both working on after dinner glasses of wine that I had ordered from the stewardess.

I told her the story. I had written the letter through the publisher as instructed. Weeks passed without a response. I had about given up. Then one day my wife called me at work to tell me I had received a strange-looking letter from someplace in Tennessee, some kind of mule farm. I told her to go ahead and open it. There was a pause, and then she said that it had something to do with Peter Cremer, that it was handwritten and hard to make out. I dropped everything and headed home. The letter was from a Marilynn Powell Greene, who introduced herself as a folk singer who raised mules. She had been touring Germany during the summer and had met Peter Cremer. After her return home, he had called and asked her to respond to my letter. He thought that it would be easier, at least initially, if one Southerner spoke to another. And yes, he would be interested in talking to me about the war.

I was floored. I digested Marilynn's letter and then, almost trembling, called her. She explained in a pert voice that a mutual friend from the German scientific community at the space center in Huntsville, Alabama, just down the road from her farm, had suggested she look Peter up while on her tour. They had hit it off, and she had spent a couple of days with him and his daughter Audrey at his North Sea island beach house. In fact, Audrey had just visited her at her farm. She explained that Peter had married late in life and that his daughter was still in college, attending the University of Wisconsin.

Marilynn went on about Peter; he was so youthful, she said so physically fit for his age — a great sense of humor and a successful businessman. He was even a consultant to NATO and did apparently secret things that he couldn't talk about.

My blond friend put down her cup of wine, enwrapped in the story.

I reached into my briefcase and pulled out the photograph of Marilynn and Peter — a woman of, perhaps, middle age, wearing a North Sea hat, stood on a beach talking to a trim man in a dark sweater and baggy striped pants.

My traveler noted, "He looks as if he might be of the age to have a daughter in college, but certainly not to have commanded a U-boat fifty years ago."

"Yes. . . . Anyway, after my conversations with Marilynn, I began talking to Peter on the phone and it led to this trip."

"That's a fascinating story," my charming listener responded. "Thank you for telling me about it. And good luck on the rest of your search!" She took the last sip from her cup of wine and picked up her magazine.

Our conversation had ended, but my finding Peter was still very much in my mind. I had doubts about what I was doing. It might have been all right to approach a man like this if I was an established writer. Certainly an incident so long ago linking my father and him possibly would not mean as much to him as it did to me. I had been quite nervous when I made the initial early morning call to Hamburg to talk to him. Would he understand me? Would I understand him? I was prepared to use my most proper, stilted English, recently developed for conversations with my foreign business acquaintances.

Suddenly, Peter Cremer was on the line from across the ocean.

He spoke with a voice shaded with a degree of accent, but very clear. I didn't know whether to call him Mister, Herr, or Commander. I had even made some notes to prompt my conversation.

"Mr. Cremer, this is Rody Johnson in Florida. Marilynn Powell Greene suggested that I call you directly. As I said in my letter, I am writing a book about my father, and possibly someone from the *Java Arrow*, and would like to include something about you."

"Yes, I have information on the *Java Arrow* that I could send to you. A picture after I torpedoed it. I would be most interested in meeting one of its crew members."

"Mr. Cremer, Marilynn said you work with Sperry Marine. Do you come to the United States? I would very much like to meet you."

"I am busy now and could not come. I have been to Florida once, to the Sperry plant."

"In Clearwater?"

He replied that he believed the city was Clearwater.

"Mr. Cremer, I would appreciate any information you might have," I responded.

"I will send it. Please make a copy and return. This history is very important."

"Yes, Sir. Thank you for the help. I enjoyed talking with you. Goodbye, Mr. Cremer."

In my excitement and nervousness I felt as if I had cut off the conversation. He seemed to have wanted to talk more. I wondered what would come of this call. Why would he send me documents and trust me to copy and return them? He certainly didn't know who I was. Marilynn probably told him I sounded OK, but still. . . .

Within two weeks a packet of papers and photographs arrived. The photographs were wonderful — aerial views of the *Java Arrow* with a hole in her side, *U-333* at sea, Cremer in uniform, and Cremer talking with a British tanker captain after the war. And there were documents, obviously research materials for his book. They included a U.S. Navy patrol boat report of an attack on a submarine off Fort Pierce that must have been *U-333*, and statements by the USS *Halsey*'s captain about the sinking of his tanker. Of particular interest was a Navy report about the *Amazone*, described as a small Dutch freighter, having been torpedoed and sunk with 14 men lost.

Two photographs in the package were puzzling. They must have been of old paintings. One looked like a castle, the other a three-masted schooner — a warship with holes for cannons along its side. Penciled notes on the back explained that the castle was Cremer's ancestral home in England, and the ship was the one his English great-grandfather, as Captain, had sailed to America in 1856. I wondered what he had in mind by sending these two pictures, which indicated an English ancestry. In addition, I was to address letters to him as Peter Cremer Thursby. The name Thursby had never been mentioned in his book.

Katharine, as an observer of all this, had said to me, "I don't know what you've gotten into, but I don't think Peter Cremer is your average U-boat commander."

Peter Cremer and I talked several times and exchanged letters. He sent me more pictures and information, all collected for his book. We became "Peter" and "Rody." I felt as if I had found a new friend — one of my father's generation — not unlike some of the men I had worked with on the vestry of my church — older men who once had financially rewarding business careers and were now retired. And while these men were successful, they were above all else gentlemen. I didn't find these types of men in my business so I gravitated towards them whenever the opportunity arose. From my conversations with Peter Cremer I felt that he fit this pattern. I sensed a gentleness and a vulnerability in him that I would not expect from a man of his stature, especially over transatlantic phone lines. Maybe it was his age; I didn't know.

I had invited Peter to come to Florida, even offered to provide the airfare. I felt uncomfortable and afraid I might insult him by my offer. But he had indicated that he was too busy to come, and I certainly didn't want to push it.

I wanted to meet Cremer and sit down and talk with him — to make true my Ocean Grill fantasy. I had accumulated sufficient frequent flyer miles from my business travels to take care of the flight. The time seemed right. I knew he was not interested in traveling to this country, and he certainly was not getting any younger. If I wanted to see him, I thought I had better go to Germany.

His voice sounded chipper over the phone. "Could I come visit over a long weekend?" I asked.

"Certainly," he replied. We picked a date, May 17. The year was 1989. He would meet me at the Hamburg Airport.

I tried to get some sleep. My seat mate sat curled up with a blanket over her. The plane droned on. The cabin lay dark except for one or two people reading. We must have been at least halfway across, somewhere on a line between Iceland and the Azores. My knees ached — no way to stretch them fully. I kept drifting off and waking up. Maybe I was getting more sleep than I thought. I hoped so. I kept thinking about meeting Peter Cremer at long last.

Chapter 9

Reinbek, Germany 1989

*J*LANDED IN Frankfurt in a daze. Saying goodbye to my seat mate, I grabbed my carry-on and left the plane. In the terminal I found a food nook and bought a croissant, an orange juice, and the *International Herald Tribune*. I sat down, nibbled on my food, and scanned the paper. On the third page I saw a brief article that the German courts had convicted a Lebanese of murder in conjunction with the hijacking of a TWA flight a few years ago. Earlier, two Germans had disappeared in the Mid-East, their kidnaping linked to the conviction. The West German Interior Minister was quoted as saying, "The risk of flying is significantly greater." I looked up from my paper and there seemed to be policemen everywhere. I hadn't noticed before.

I finished my breakfast and wandered around until I found the gate for the connection to Hamburg. I plopped down in a seat, folded the paper in my lap, and shut my eyes. I had two hours until flight time.

The man at the counter announced in German what I presumed was the departure of the flight to Hamburg. I stood up and followed the crowd, which did not board the plane through the jet way but walked down some steps and filed out onto the tarmac. There spread out in front of the 727 lay suitcases, bags, and boxes. I figured out that I had to first identify my bags before they and I were allowed to board the plane. The German authorities obviously took this terrorism thing seriously. I found my bags and showed the policeman my baggage stubs; he nodded, and I climbed up the portable stairway into the plane.

Settling into my seat, I closed my eyes and remembered a model of a Navy fighter plane that my father helped me build out of balsa wood and tissue paper, painted with dope to make the paper stretch tight over the frame. I kept it hung from an overhead light in my room for a while then took it outside, lit the tail with a match, threw it up in the air, and watched it crash to the ground and burn in a flash.

The next image that came into my mind was an incident that had happened in 1943. A gray Navy dive bomber was coming in low on approach to the Vero Beach airport for a landing — descending over the houses, a block down the street from where I stood. I was at a Cub Scout meeting, playing in the den mother's front yard with several other boys. I looked up and saw the pilot and the gunner silhouetted through the cockpit canopy against the blue sky. Suddenly the bomber dipped its wing, hooked a power line, and flipped into the street. It stood on its nose tail up, tottering. The engine exploded — red and yellow flames shot up the fuselage. The plane toppled on its side. I couldn't run. I couldn't yell. I stared. I had seen planes crash in the news reels, but this was real.

The roar swept down the street and crashed over me like a wave. I heard the den mother scream. As she dragged me into her house, I looked over my shoulder at black smoke rising into the sky.

I shook my head, clearing the tragedy from my mind. I picked up the paper and began to read while the jet lifted off the runway at Frankfurt.

As I stepped from the plane in Hamburg, my first thought was, would I recognize Peter when I saw him? I began peering at every man I passed. I was tired and nervous. I was hardly in the best of shape to meet the man I had been obsessed to find for two years.

I waited at the baggage pick-up, lifted my bags off the conveyor, and watched while the passengers on my flight grabbed their luggage and left. After a few minutes I stood alone in an empty terminal. No Peter Cremer.

We had faxed messages, and he was to recognize me by my yellow sweater. I certainly had seen enough pictures of him. I began to wonder what I should do.

A single figure approached across the empty baggage area. He strode towards me — a lean man with black hair, a weathered face with age marks, smiling, clad in a gray shirt with snaps for buttons and shoulder epaulets, and baggy blue trousers. He carried a leather jacket over his arm. I had expected a business executive, and he looked like a seaman.

"Rody, I'm glad you are here!" He didn't hesitate in his recognition; he stretched out his hand which I grasped immediately.

"Peter, I appreciate you picking me up."

"No difficulty. I'm sorry you had to wait. I couldn't find a parking place." Grabbing my bags, he led the way out of the dim terminal into a bright spring day. He waved me towards a double-parked, brown Mercedes sports coupe, of not-too-recent vintage and tossed my bags into the trunk, shoving a set of golf clubs out of the way. I slipped into the worn, front seat. Peter pulled out of the airport and maneuvered with authority through the stop-and-go streets of Hamburg toward the suburban town of Reinbek where he lived.

We chatted easily about my trip, the weather in Florida and Hamburg — suddenly comfortable with each other after our phone calls of the last few months. It seemed like a long time until we were out in the country and racing along the autobahn. As Peter whipped off the freeway at the Reinbek exit I thought, this guy drives like he's in the Grand Prix. He geared down as we entered an immaculate little town and took me into the hotel at the town center. "After you have rested, I will pick you up, and we will have tea in the Bismarck Forest," he said.

Peter came by an hour later. I had shaved and showered, and we took a brief ride to an inn surrounded by woods. Peter told me that it had been originally a corn mill that dated back to 1350, and then later owned by Prince Otto von Bismarck after he had acquired the property in 1871. The mill had been converted to a two-story hotel and restaurant with a red peaked roof and dormer windows.

The innkeeper greeted Peter warmly at the front door and ushered us through the dining room to a balcony overlooking the water wheel on a mill pond, with ducks quacking to a background of rustling water. We sat at a table where the late afternoon sun shone on Peter's face. He smiled with enjoyment and ordered tea and cheesecake. I wanted a beer after my all-night flight. But Peter insisted that I order what he had, and told me I would not regret it. The cake tasted light and delicious, and we stirred sweet sticks in the tea. I began to feel refreshed. The dullness in my head disappeared.

After our tea, he guided me on a walk from the inn along a path into the woods. The trees grew in rows, as if they had been planted that way years ago. The canopy from their leaves shut out the light that had been so pleasant on the porch. The woods lay dark and ominous as the air turned cold in the dusk. Peter wanted to show me the wild boar and deer that ran free in the forest and seemed disappointed when he couldn't produce them for his guest.

We returned to the inn and to the paneled bar with its deer and boar head mounts. I felt the warmth from logs burning brightly in a stone fireplace. We enjoyed a dinner of roast beef strips, salad, and a beer. The owner's Newfoundland dog put his massive head in my lap, and I scratched his ears while Peter and I talked. We stayed away from Peter's wartime exploits. That would wait until tomorrow.

As Peter was telling me about the history of Bismarck's ownership of the surrounding area, I realized something that had been puzzling me all during dinner. Peter looked, even seemed, familiar, and I couldn't place who he reminded me of. Then it struck — my Uncle Howard — his smile, his eyes, his lean features were similar. This discovery must have shown on my face.

"Rody, are you all right?" Peter asked.

"Oh. Yes, I'm fine. It just dawned on me that you remind me of my Uncle Howard, my father's twin brother."

"That's good." There was a twinkle in Peter's eye. "Was he a navy man, too?"

"As a matter of fact, he was. Commanded a minesweeper in the Mediterranean and later in the Pacific."

"That's a tough business. What did he do after the war?" asked Peter.

"He became president of the family business, a company that sold electrical equipment to the mines in West Virginia," I replied.

"And your father, what did he do?"

"He started a sporting goods business in Florida."

"I find it interesting what people do after their war experiences," he commented as he took a sip of his coffee.

"My dad, when he was finally taken into the regular Coast Guard, commanded an old houseboat running patrols along the Florida Gulf Coast. After a while, I think he was bored. There was no action. He had plenty of time by 1944 to consider what he would do after the war."

Peter remarked, "I cannot say we were ever bored; scared, yes. There was no time to think of the future. We were just trying to survive each day at that point."

Peter finished his coffee, we walked out into the crisp evening air and got into his Mercedes for the ride back to the hotel. I now felt quite tired. The trip had caught up with me. We drove without talking. Suddenly, I heard Peter say, "Here we are, Rody. I will see you in the morning."

"Thank you, Peter. It's been a wonderful evening." I walked into the lobby of the hotel. In my room I took off my clothes, brushed my teeth, and dropped into bed. Peter was everything I had anticipated. I looked forward to what tomorrow would bring, but fell asleep in mid-thought.

At eight the next morning I woke up, dressed, and went down to the lobby and outside to check the day — the air felt cool, the sky clear. I looked forward to spending the day with Peter. I felt great, my night's sleep having wiped away all sense of jet lag. I ate breakfast and then explored Reinbek.

The hotel sat in the middle of a small business district with store fronts that were lined with shrubs and flower boxes. Three roads intersected at the hotel's front, all joining together and heading downhill toward the train station and a lake beyond. A stream ran along the edge of the town center. Up the hill, a couple of blocks from the hotel, sat a stone 19th-century church with flying buttresses. Tree-lined residential streets surrounded the town.

At that hour on a Saturday morning, the most popular spot in town was the bakery. Cars double-parked as a stream of people flowed in and out of the shop. The smell of bread permeated the air as I walked by. The town reminded me of a suburban community in the U.S., even like downtown Vero Beach used to be. I would get to know Reinbek well, walking the streets and going into the shops during the three days I was there. Outside the hotel no one spoke English, but I managed. Once I ended up with two ice cream cones instead of the double dipper that I thought I had ordered.

At 11:00 a.m., Peter picked me up in front of the hotel. "I must go by the market. You don't mind, do you?"

"Certainly not. It sounds like fun." I felt good and the day added to the feeling. I was enjoying this man and the place where he lived, and wanted to savor every minute of it.

Racing his Mercedes through the quiet residential streets, Peter came to a large parking area full of BMWs, VWs, and Mercedes. He grabbed two baskets from the back seat and strode forth enthusiastically toward a line of trees. I had trouble keeping up. From sheds and stalls tucked in between the trees Peter, working from a list, filled his baskets with bananas, apples, parsley, and jam. We returned to the car and drove a few blocks to his home.

The house stood back from the street, rising two stories, with a peaked roof and tall trees standing on either side, looking as if it belonged on a Bavarian postcard. The house had been built in 1936. We entered through the kitchen, where a young man bent over the sink washing dishes.

"This is my son Marc," said Peter. "He is home for a few days from his studies at the university in Bonn." Marc, a handsome fellow, smiled, and we shook hands. I could only think that he was younger than three of my four children, one of whom also was named Mark, yet this young man's father had to be at least my mother's age.

Peter led me through a paneled dining room into a bright, high-ceilinged parlor with large windows opening on the backyard. Portraits of every conceivable size, arranged in what appeared to be family tree order, covered the walls, as if in a museum. I stared in amazement at the paintings.

"These are my ancestors," Peter informed me, his eyes twinkling. "I can trace my family in England back to 1200. There is a large house there that is now a museum that belonged to my family. I have visited it. It is in Abington near Oxford. This is the Thursby coat of arms." He pointed to a framed emblem.

I knew about coats of arms. My mother had a couple hanging on the wall when I was a child. But the best we could date back to was the 1600s when an ancestor killed a duke in Ireland — for a good cause, of course — and then fled to America to pioneer western Virginia.

The Thursby name had confused me. In Peter's letters, the stationery heading was Peter Cremer Thursby. As we looked at the portraits of his family, I asked about this name.

"Yes, I changed my name several years ago. It is my father's mother's family name. She was English."

He explained that his grandmother was a Thursby, and her father, his great-grandfather, had been in the Royal Navy, and was the one who had sailed to the United States in the 1850s. As a child Peter had visited his grandmother's family in England. His interest in the sea went back to this ancestor in the British navy. His father told him about his great-grand-father's naval career. Peter grew up seeing pictures of his great-grandfather and his naval decorations.

We proceeded from the living room down a couple of steps into a study, its walls covered with books — a bright room with French doors that led out to a patio and an enclosed back yard. Nowhere did I see any sign of Peter's war activities.

"Let us sit outside. It is a beautiful day," suggested Peter.

We walked out into the yard, pulled together a couple of lawn chairs by a table, and settled in for a chat that must have lasted three hours. Peter wore his sunglasses and had rolled his long-sleeved shirt back at the wrists. Loaded with a camera, a small tape recorder, and my legal pad full of questions, I felt nervous but ready to begin the long-awaited interview. The freshness of the spring day, the smell of flowers, birds chirping in the surrounding trees, and Peter's quick smile relaxed me. Only the peal of church bells in town announcing non-stop afternoon weddings interrupted our talk. Marc, with his kitchen duties finished, had come out on the patio and stretched out in the sun reading.

Not on my list, but driven by my confusion from talking about his English background and thinking that certainly he had been born in Germany, I asked, "Peter, were you raised in Hamburg?"

"No, France."

My face must have shown even more surprise, because he kept talking, explaining.

"I was born in Lorraine. The Germans and French fought for centuries over Alsace-Lorraine. Since 1871, it had been German. But it is very French. My mother's family was French. I went to a French school. In our family we never spoke German. If you speak German, the shop keep-er won't give you the best." He then told me that his grandfather had taken him to the huge World War I monument at Verdun when he was a boy.

I had to think about all this for a moment. Peter was born before World

War I when Lorraine was part of Germany. A few years later, France won it back. Well, if his mother was French and the territory where the family lived kept bouncing back and forth between France and Germany, then his father must have been German.

"No, my father was born in France. His mother was English as I have mentioned, his father of Dutch origin. I can show you the pedigree. My father died when I was fourteen. He was very stiff. He was president of a court, like a judge in your country." Peter hesitated, then laughed. "With my background, English, French with a German citizenship, I could have been a spy."

"I'll say, but how did you end up in the German navy?" I asked.

"I had a German nationality. The German navy's traditions are the same as the English Navy traditions. They evolved from the English."

The family plan was for Peter to go to Grenoble University in France and study law like his father. But he wanted to go into the German navy. Even with his German citizenship, he was having difficulty being accepted by the German Naval Academy because of his varied background. Then, he got a break. The academy's sailing ship had sunk during a training exercise. With many of the cadets lost at sea, openings to the academy had become more readily available. But he still had needed help. "Admiral Raeder pulled strings to get me in," Peter explained. Admiral Erich Raeder later became commander of the German navy under Hitler. Peter had entered the academy in 1932, the year before the Reichstag gave Hitler dictatorial powers.

I digested all this, made a note on my pad, and then asked, "What about your nickname, 'Ali'?" I knew from his book that he had been called this.

"It was for crazy King Alaric who had fought against the Romans. I got it in the navy. My friends think I am also a crazy man," he said, smiling.

"I read the story about when you and some other submarine officers had been invited to Admiral Doenitz's headquarters for dinner. Apparently you thought the Admiral's food dull so you and a friend raided a German army officer's mess, got caught by the military police, let the air out of the police's tires, escaped, and presented the food to the Admiral. Is that why you got your nickname?"

"I suppose," he said, still smiling.

I had read the story about the food raid in the book about submarine commanders that I had found in a library two years earlier.

U-333's officers stand in the damaged conning tower as it docks at La Rochelle, France. The
"Three Little Fishies" insignia is painted on the side. Commander Peter Cremer, in the white
hat, stands under the bent periscope.   *Peter*

King Alaric, I later discovered had been the leader of the Visigoths, a merry band of mercenaries who roamed the Roman Empire causing havoc in the time of Atilla the Hun. Alaric sacked Rome in 410, but died at the age of 40. Both the original Ali and his modern namesake had been dashing young warriors, but Peter had had better luck in surviving his war.

"Peter, how in the world did you come up with the 'Three Little Fishies' insignia for your submarine? That's an American song. I remember it as a child."

"I know," said Peter, laughing. "In Paris, before your country was in the war, I knew an American girl. She had nice parties; we listened to her records. One was 'Three Little Fishies.' It fit the *U-333* boat number. It had a note of 'don't worry, don't take things too seriously.' I thought it would be good for the crew — make them forget about depth charges. I had the record the girl gave me on my boat. She was a nurse for the Red Cross. I don't know what happened to her. I guess she must have returned to the United States before you got into the war."

He went on to say that this American girl had heard that the Germans were advancing on Paris and thought it her duty to go outside the city and warn the French troops. She stood on a road and waved at some tanks rolling by, yelling to them, "Be careful the Germans are coming!" The tanks were German. The story tickled Peter.

Continuing, I asked Peter about the U.S. Navy report that said that the *Java Arrow* had been hit by a torpedo on the port side and 30 seconds later on the starboard side. How could this be? Were there two U-boats involved in the attack? Peter declared: "Absolutely not! The report was wrong."

After our meeting, I discovered a U.S. Navy report and the log of *U-109* while doing research in the National Archives. The report stated that *U-333*'s second torpedo had hit the tip of the stern and could have given a rattled tanker crew the impression that it exploded on the starboard side. But, indeed, a second U-boat had been in the area, and she had fired a torpedo at the drifting *Java Arrow* several hours after *U-333*'s attack, according to *U-109*'s log. This sub had been in the Cape Canaveral area during the early days of May 1942. I had that portion of her log translated.

Continuing to verify information I had found, I asked Peter about a story told by a crewman from the tanker USS *Halsey*. This fellow was in a lifeboat in the early morning after the *Halsey* had been torpedoed by

USS Halsey, down at the bow, after having been torpedoed by U-333 the same night as the USS Java Arrow and the SS Amazone, May 6, 1942. The tanker was owned by Farr Spinning Company, Wilmington, Delaware.

U-333. He claimed a German submarine had come alongside and the commander had tossed a bottle of scotch and a *Miami Herald* into the life boat.

Peter laughed at that one. He related a similar experience, "Off Greenland, after sinking a Norwegian ship, we surfaced and showed the men in one of the lifeboats how to head for Newfoundland. But we would never do that so close to the Florida coast. I admire people like your *Halsey* crewman but they tell funny stories."

Of course this discussion was heading toward the one story that I really wanted Peter to verify. "Peter, my father, while he was in the Coast Guard Auxiliary, ran up on three German subs off Bethel Shoal a couple of months after the *Java Arrow* rescue. Why would three subs be together? Were they exchanging supplies?"

"It could not have happened. It would be too dangerous. There was no need. The 'Milch Cows' — the large submarines that furnished provisions and fuel to German fleet submarines at sea — provided supplies to each boat just as they did for my boat. Rody, would you excuse me for a moment, I will show you something."

Peter got up and went inside the house. I was disappointed. I believed my dad's story. I had heard it for years. True, there hadn't been many details until I had talked to Ottie, but he certainly remembered that night clearly. Who was I to believe?

Peter returned carrying a large framed picture. Proudly he held it up for me to see. Admiral Doenitz stood in full navy regalia, arms crossed, staring at the camera. At the bottom of the picture, written on the mat, was an extensive inscription.

"He gave this picture to me when I was working on his staff in 1943 after I was wounded," Peter explained. He broke into a smile.

"One morning I arrived at his 8 a.m. staff meeting a little tipsy. The great Admiral knew it and asked me for my report. I replied, 'Commander Cremer has nothing to report today, Sir.'"

Peter laughed, enjoying the memory. He went on to tell me that Doenitz had lived near Reinbek, and that other U-boat commanders including himself, "old companions" as he put it, had looked after Doenitz's wife while the Admiral had served his ten-year sentence imposed by the Nuremberg war crimes trials. "She was an old lady who didn't know about his situation," he said. At Doenitz's funeral in 1980, Peter had held the plaque with the Admiral's war decorations on it.

Peter Cremer holding a photo of Admiral Karl Doenitz in 1989. Cremer had worked on Doenitz's staff while recuperating from wounds after his sub, *U-333*, had been attacked in October 1942.   *Peter Cremer*

Showing me Doenitz's picture and the mention of the Nuremberg trials took our conversation away from his background and experiences into a broader, more political sphere. Peter apparently felt it necessary to say something on that pleasant afternoon that will stay with me and cause questions in my mind the rest of my life.

"A British naval officer who interrogated me after I surrendered at the end of the war told me about the concentration camps. He was Jewish, had a bald head and a big nose, but I liked him. We became friends. But you cannot fight if you know these things. I didn't believe him, the killing of the Jews."

I sat there thinking about Peter Cremer's background — more French and English than German. Yet, he had committed himself to a German naval career and had ended up fighting against his "mother" countries. How could he have done this? I didn't ask the question; I was afraid to. It seemed impolite, in that setting, to question my host about sensitive subjects.

Later, I would try to rationalize Peter's war career. I could relate it somewhat to an experience of my own. I had been assigned to a development project of a communications system for the small ICBM (Intercontinental Ballistic Missile). I had mixed feelings about missiles that carried nuclear warheads. I knew of engineers who refused to work on such projects. And yet, I had worked on this one. The purpose of the project had been lost in the challenge and excitement of accomplishment.

I had pushed my conscience aside. Maybe Peter had done the same thing. I didn't feel that I had to work on the project out of duty for my country, as perhaps Peter did in fighting a war for the country of his nationality. Of course, he had gone into the German navy before Hitler became dictator. What I wanted to believe, longed to believe, was that Peter Cremer had nothing to do with the Nazis. But when I told friends about him I could see them saying to themselves, "Sure, who are you kidding?" In most people's minds, if he served under Hitler, he was a Nazi.

As wrapped up as I was in Peter, I did question how he could have not known about the German treatment of the Jews. I worked this out to some degree by reading about the Nuremberg trials. Admiral Doenitz had been sentenced for his wartime activities. That trial had found no link between Doenitz and the Jewish situation. Although he had replaced Hitler as the head of Germany during the last few days of the war, the tribunal judged him a navy officer who prepared for and fought a war, not as a government official who knew of the atrocities. If this was true of Doenitz, it could also be true of Peter. But I would continue to have doubts that would never be totally erased. Peter said he could not have fought if he had known, but fight he did.

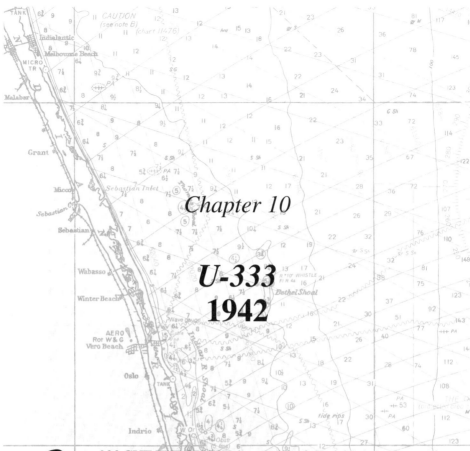

Chapter 10

U-333
1942

U-333 CUT THROUGH the swells of the mid-Atlantic at 11 knots, its long, narrow hull pitching slightly. On the cramped bridge Lieutenant Commander Peter Cremer stood looking at the bare horizon, enjoying the blue rolling sea and a cloudless sky. His white Commander's hat shaded his eyes. He felt a slight warmth to the air, the first sign, he thought, of his boat's destination, the Florida coast. The U-boat's diesels vibrated smoothly under him. On the bridge with him stood four lookouts. Below, the remainder of his crew worked in split shifts — one shift on duty, the other sleeping.

The date was April 20, 1942, the day *U-333* was to meet with the "Milch Cow" supply submarine. A coded radio message from U-boat headquarters in France gave them the coordinates for the rendezvous. They had been at sea 20 days and had covered almost 4,000 miles. Except for the attack by a British bomber off the French coast and one of the diesels quitting, the trip had been quiet. Both incidents could have ended the mission.

The bomber had surprised them two hours out from their bomb-

U-333, commanded by Peter Cremer.

Peter Cremer

The German U-boat *U-333* running on the surface.

proof bunker at La Rochelle, France. It was rare for the Royal Air Force to be that far from home. Cremer's crew had responded well, and the quick emergency dive had saved the boat from serious damage. The engine breakdown had frustrated Cremer as they sat rocking on the surface for two days. He knew he was not helping by constantly asking for progress reports. But Chief Mechanic Heber did his job. After replacing a cylinder liner and changing a piston, they were underway again.

A seaman came up through the hatch and handed Cremer an inventory of needed supplies and a fuel reading. He acknowledged with a nod and then stepped back on the gun platform, ducking under the barrel of the antiaircraft gun to review the list. He took a minute to lean on the safety rail and look out over the stern and the wake tailing behind. Fortunately, Allied aircraft didn't have the range to cover this part of the Atlantic; if they did, *U-333* would be a clear target.

Cremer thought about the United States and what lay ahead, wondering if the coast still remained lit up and if the U.S. Navy still remained unable to protect these waters. He visualized in his mind the charts of his destination — the eastern coast of central Florida south of Cape Canaveral.

A few of the other U-boat Commanders, Cremer knew, had good success on their missions to the far shore, sinking three and four ships. He wanted to surpass that. He had 17 torpedoes on board, 3 above normal capacity. But nothing was normal about this voyage. *U-333* was a Type VII-C boat built for excursions out into the Atlantic, not transoceanic voyages. The 120 tons of diesel fuel she carried gave her a 9,000-mile range. The roundtrip to Florida of 8,000 miles, plus two weeks of operations to find and sink ships, did not leave much margin for error. Cremer was grateful that he was being resupplied.

"Milch Cow at 30 degrees," sounded the starboard lookout. Cremer saw the large conning tower and bulky hull of the supply submarine approaching. He brought more of the crew on deck to handle lines, fuel hoses, and to pass below the additional food and spare parts.

The two U-boats took up positions parallel to each other on the quiet sea. A hose on floats connected the boats across the open water, and an inflatable rubber dinghy was rowed back and forth hauling supplies. The transfer was made without incident, and as the supply sub pulled away, Cremer gave its captain an appreciative wave.

After the Milch Cow's departure, Cremer went below, replaced by his Number One. He climbed down the ladder through the conning tower to the control room, where four men were on duty. He went aft through the engineers' quarters and past the four bunks, two high, on each side where the men off watch slept until their watch changed. Snores mixed with the sound of the engines. Cremer went into the galley and poured himself a cup of coffee from a pot sitting next to the two-burner stove.

Cremer liked to tour his boat periodically. He opened the bulkhead door to the engine room and stuck his head inside. The noise of the diesels hammered his ears, the smell of engine fumes filled his nose. Beyond the diesels were the electric motors and the single stern torpedo tube. He waved at the Chief Engineer, knew things were under control, and closed the door.

Retracing his steps, he passed back through the engineers' quarters and, before reentering the control room, checked the aft head. He opened the door and saw sausages hanging from the ceiling and boxes of food piled on the seat and squeezed into every corner — items just received from the Milch Cow. The smells of the meat and the ripening vegetables penetrated his nose. He closed the door. Back to one head again, he thought. With the length of the journey, they had no choice. Within ten days the food would be used up, and the toilet would be available once more. In the meantime, 55 men would use the forward head — not a desirable ratio.

Cremer passed through the control room, picked up the log, and stepped over the bulkhead door into the officers' quarters. Cubby holes, first for the radio room and then the sound location room were on his right. Immediately to his left were his quarters. He pulled back a curtain and sat down at a small table, not much bigger than a tray. The arrangement was so tight that he had to fold up the table and seat when he climbed into his bunk. He placed the log and his coffee on the table, took a pen from his vest pocket, and entered the day's report. In the next compartment, the ward room, two of his off-duty officers sat opposite each other on their bunks playing cards on a fold-up table. One turned his head and asked, "Everything well, Captain?"

"Absolutely, Rheinholt," replied Cremer, smiling.

Later, he would check forward. The next compartment was the chief rates's quarters, one double-decker bunk on each side and a collapsible mess table. The forward head stood on the port side next to the bulkhead door to the torpedo room. Cremer felt compassion for the crew in there with three double-decker bunks on each side and the three extra torpedoes lashed to the deck in between. The four bow tubes filled the forward part of the room. The crew assigned to these quarters ate sitting on the bunks balancing their trays on the torpedoes. They would be glad to shoot the tube torpedoes and replace them with those on the deck.

After making the last entry in the log, he sat back and rested his head against the bulkhead, closing his eyes. The air in the cabin smelled almost fresh, being sucked in from the outside as they ran on the surface, a pleasant switch from the submerged atmosphere — a mixture of body, ripe vegetable, fuel oil, electrical, and cooking odors. It took one's nose time to adjust.

Thoughts slipped through his mind. It had been six months since *U-333* had been commissioned and he had taken command. The first mission off Greenland in the early winter had been a success of sorts. They had sunk four ships, but the fourth had been the SS *Spreewald*, a German ship, running the Allied blockade. He didn't like to think about that one. When the *U-333* had arrived home at the dock at La Rochelle, there were no greeters, no bands, and no flowers to celebrate a successful mission. Instead, Cremer was yanked off his boat and taken to Admiral Doenitz's headquarters for immediate interrogation. His career was on the line. From childhood he had wanted to be a naval officer — now, he faced courtmartial. If he did not defend himself well, he probably would be transferred to the army and sent to the Russian front. But he believed in Admiral Doenitz.

Of course, he had sunk the ship. She had been disguised as a British cargo passenger vessel, the *Ena*. He had not been informed that she existed; she was off course; and she did not report her position. The German High Command demanded that responsibility be placed. His Admiral listened to the facts, stood up to his superiors, and refused to allow one of his men to be blamed unjustly. Cremer was returned to *U-333*. After the frigid North Atlantic and the *Spreewald* incident, he thought the Florida mission would be a vacation.

From his cramped seat, Cremer stretched his legs out under the table and chuckled. He wondered if Doenitz had received that bill from the restaurant in Paris. And Doenitz had financed the trip to Paris anyway — had given him 4,000 francs when he and some other U-boat commanders were dining at Doenitz's headquarters. He had requested orders to go to Paris with a cock-and-bull story about checking up on some junior officers who were there on leave. Doenitz told them to go. Cremer admitted he didn't have any money. That's when the Admiral gave him an advance.

Cremer had a marvelous time and had spent everything. On the last night, he was with three elegant but slightly older French women, in a fancy restaurant. He remembered the bleached blond stroking his hand and asking, "Won't they bring us more champagne, Baby Sailor?"

Cremer knew he looked young, but didn't appreciate the "Baby Sailor" bit. He called the maitre d' over who, instead of providing more champagne, demanded payment. Cremer took out his card and wrote down the Admiral's address and told him to send the bill there.

The maitre d', taking the card, asked, "What will the Admiral do to you?"

"I hope to be far away when he receives this," he answered.

Two weeks after the refueling by the Milch Cow, Cremer stood on the bridge in semi-darkness. His boat lay ten miles off the Florida coast, a shoreline that glowed with the lights of what showed on his chart as the towns of Melbourne, Vero Beach, and Fort Pierce. He and his crew were flabbergasted; they had come from a blacked-out Europe where one cupped his hand to hide the flare of a match when lighting a cigarette. They could not believe that the Americans even had their lighthouses operating. He had seen the beacon sweeping the sea from Cape Canaveral. And the Bethel Shoal buoy sat nearby, its gas light blinking.

With that glow from the coast, all he had to do was lay outside the shipping lanes, watch for the silhouettes of the ships to pass, and fire away — just like a shooting gallery. Everything was perfect except for the condition of his boat, resulting from yet another incident. Cremer wondered if he was jinxed. *U-333* had been rammed by a tanker off Bermuda. The collision could have not only ended the trip but sent the sub to the bottom of the ocean.

How had he let himself get into that predicament? The tanker was zig-zagging, the setting sun making the visibility difficult. He wanted to

U-333 returning to La Rochelle, France, May 1942. A tanker had rammed the sub off Bermuda, damaging part of its bridge and periscope, and crushing its bow.
Peter Cremer

position *U-333* so that the tanker couldn't see her. He missed with the first two torpedoes. Submerged, he stalked the tanker and finally got into position to fire again. He raised the periscope and saw the huge, dark shape of the ship bearing down on him. The tanker had turned on *U-333*.

Cremer had screamed, "Dive! Dive!" but it was too late. The tanker rode over the submarine like a freight train with a screeching, scraping sound of metal that he would never forget. The boat lost power momentarily, water poured in from cracks in the stern plates. He yelled the command to surface to assess the damage. The conning tower hatch had jammed, so he climbed on deck through the emergency hatch in the galley. By then, it had become dark, and he could see the outline of the tanker moving off toward the east.

The submarine's damage consisted of a crushed bow, part of the bridge knocked off, a periscope that looked like a bent curtain rod, two of the four forward torpedo tube caps jammed, the direction finder and torpedo aiming device on the bridge destroyed, and leaks in the stern. Luckily, the diesels and electric motors were fine. Cremer could maneuver, but had no periscope to see where he was going while submerged, limiting him to surface attacks only. He had two bow tubes operational and would have to take the time to reload for a third shot or turn the boat around and fire the single stern torpedo.

Once again, the sub had drifted on the surface while the chief mechanic and his engine crew worked miracles with a blowtorch and fixed what they could. Cremer built a sighting device on the bridge out of a set of binoculars so that he could aim the whole boat and fire the two good tubes. However, he believed that he had made the right decision to proceed, not to return to France. They had come too far to turn back. He wrote in his log: "Intention — ahead into the Straits of Florida. In no circumstances return home without steamer."

The next night just before midnight, *U-333* lay silently on the surface, the sea lapping against the hull, the Bethel Shoal buoy blinking to the west. From below, the hydrophone operator reported engine noises from an approaching ship. Within a few minutes Cremer, standing on the bridge, spotted the dark form. It looked like a big tanker. He worried that a quarter moon would soon crack the eastern horizon outlining the submarine's shape, but he had to take the risk that the tanker wouldn't see him until after he had fired the torpedoes.

Cremer positioned his boat to the east and lined her up on the target, a

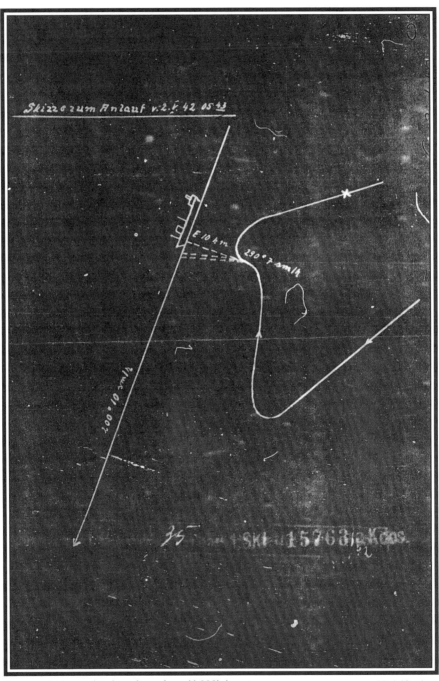

The attack plot on the *Java Arrow* from *U-333's* log.   *Mark Mondano*

silhouette slowly moving against the backdrop of the lighted coast. His heart pounded as it always did just before an attack. He sighted through the make-shift binocular targeting device that had replaced the one destroyed off Bermuda. He spoke through the bridge tube to the control room, providing information that would be fed into the attack computer.

"Large tanker, inside course south. Prepare for attack. Set torpedo depth at ten feet, torpedo speed thirty knots, tanker speed ten knots. Bow position left 90 degrees, estimated distance one mile." The minutes ticked by.

"Range 700 yards. Range 600 yards. Fire tube one."

Cremer felt the boat recoil as the torpedo launched. He watched 30 seconds tick past on his watch.

"Fire tube two." Cremer tracked the phosphorous wake of the first torpedo and watched it strike the tanker midships. Less than a minute later a dull thud ricocheted back across the water. He saw the second torpedo hit the stern, followed by a burst of flame. Good shot, he said to himself.

Cremer watched, then spoke into the tube, "Tanker burning, hit engine room."

A few minutes passed as he waited to assure *U-333*'s success. He reported, "Being abandoned by crew. Stern is under water. Tanker sinking."

Chapter 11

Success
1989

*A*S THE SHADOWS spread across his back yard, and the late afternoon sun dipped behind the trees, Peter talked about his life and career after the war and his years with Phillips Electronics and his current position with Sperry Marine.

"My job was to grow the business in Germany. I was successful, but it was what you call a rat race. After the war, the only job I can find is working on the Hamburg docks, discharging and loading ships. I am paid in cigarettes. I am selling the cigarettes to the prostitutes so I can have money. Finally in desperation I went to England to seek help from my relatives."

I thought that for a proud man to ask for help had to have been difficult. With almost an embarrassed smile, Peter continued. "I went to my uncle's house. I was greeted at the door by the butler. He showed me in. I was hungry. I sat at the dining room table in my ragged clothes. My uncle was in formal dress. I was fed and stayed overnight. The butler asked what water temperature to draw for my bath. But the family had no inclination to help someone find work who had been the enemy."

On that trip, however, a British naval officer had helped Peter get work with British Petroleum — the same officer who had been his interrogator and who had told him about the concentration camps.

"He said that I was a nice man but had fought on the wrong side," Peter explained.

Peter went on. "I worked in the oil fields, then in a refinery. I was told if I wanted a higher job you must wait, but I don't want to wait. I made three times more salary by going to work for Phillips. I worked my way up the ranks to become Managing Director of Phillips' defense business in Germany."

He had managed several plants and 2,000 people.

"Peter, how did you end up with Sperry Marine?" I figured most men his age would have retired long ago.

He answered, "It was time to retire from Phillips, but I must have a job to send my children, Marc and Audrey, to the university. I knew of Sperry through my work at Phillips. They offered me a position as manager of their Hamburg office. The company manufactures electronics for both commercial and naval ships. I still had my navy connections. Once I was involved in the sale of sonar equipment to a German company that built submarines for Norway. Because I had been on a destroyer during the German invasion of Norway, I was not allowed by the Norwegians to enter their country."

He may have been shunned by former enemies, but not at home. I was told later by one of his Sperry associates that when they had business conferences with the German navy, Peter's reputation was such that the officers would snap to attention when he entered the room.

Peter had also been limited in his travels because of his security clearance. He could not drive to Berlin; the possibility being that he could have been detained by the East Germans and that they might elicit secret information from him.

Peter explained, "The Russians are twenty-five miles away. Wake up in the morning and they are here. We can't give up the arms. Gorbachev is mostly 'public relations,' but people in Germany want to believe that the Russians are no longer to be feared." His statements, of course, were made prior to the dismantling of the Berlin Wall in 1989.

Peter had faced other security fears as well. In the late '70s and early '80s, when the American military placed Pershing missiles with nuclear warheads on German soil, a strong anti-American feeling had prevailed. Sperry's office worried that they might have a terrorist bomb attack.

"I would drive to the office and pull my Mercedes into a lift which took it to an upper level parking area. One day a bomb went off in a garage nearby. It could have been targeted at me, a German working for an American business," said Peter.

I checked my watch. It was after four. We had talked for three hours in Peter's back yard, and I had run out of questions. It had been an exhilarating afternoon except for Peter not believing or verifying my dad's story of the three subs. Peter gave me a ride back to the hotel and stated he would pick me up at six for dinner.

In my hotel room, I flopped down on the bed and turned on the TV, then flipped it off. I thought about Peter working on the docks surrounded by the devastation of Hamburg at the end of the war, struggling to survive, but with talents to offer, as the European economy eventually revived itself. My dad came out of the war to an economy that quickly boomed. He had an idea for a business that would take advantage of the pent-up demand for recreation that had been suppressed by the Depression and then the war. Dad thought people from all over the country would come to Vero Beach to enjoy the hunting and fishing — quail and turkey in the back country; ducks on the marsh; black bass in the canals and lakes; snook, trout, and tarpon in the Indian River; and sailfish offshore.

The Florida Sporting Goods had been located on a corner of U.S. 1 between downtown Vero Beach and the new Miracle Mile shopping center to the east. Lying on that hotel bed in Reinbek I could see the white, curved front building that Dad had built, with its large, recessed display windows. I remembered the inside expanse filled with athletic equipment, fishing tackle, rifles and shotguns, a sailing dinghy, a runabout boat with an outboard motor on its stern, a blown-up rubber raft, and Schwinn bicycles. My mother jokingly called it the Florida Sporting House, a reference to the only sport it did not seem to cover. If that store building existed today, it would still be one of the most modern in town.

I thought about how excited I had been the day Branch Rickey and his Brooklyn Dodger baseball players browsed in the store, when they had first come to Vero for spring training in 1948. Mr. Rickey had fished with Dad, and once had advised me on what kind of catcher's mitt to buy from the store's stock.

However, the out-of-town clientele didn't materialize in sufficient numbers, as Dad had thought, to sustain the guide and charter service, and Vero was too small a market on its own. The postwar demand had worked in a different way. The marshes were drained as agriculture expanded, and access to the back country and its fishing and hunting country became more difficult. Developers bulkheaded the shoreline as the town grew, and the saltwater fishing began to deteriorate.

To compensate, Dad did innovative things. He added an air boat to whisk fisherman and duck hunters to fishing holes and blinds in the marsh. He sold war-surplus rubber rafts before rafts became popular. He and I hooked a big lemon shark off the beach out of one of those rafts. He may have been the first person to put twin outboard motors on boats. I still have old photographs of his experiment streaking down the river. He sold Whizzer motor bikes and gave me one as a teenager, hoping every kid in town would want one. However, I had talked to my friends about the way mine broke down and killed the market. I was 15 and worked in the store part-time for 35 cents an hour. For the next several years the store just hung on.

Dad realized that he had created an "Abercrombie & Fitch" in a small town that couldn't afford it. Discouragement came in the form of five-dollar sales days in the slow, hot summer month of August. He would disappear in the afternoons, and I knew that his jeep would be parked downtown at the gas station — that he had gone to the picture show to escape the store and the heat.

Dad's business career seemed so opposite from that of the men I admired. Peter had achieved success by becoming a managing director of a division of a large corporation. And while Dad struggled with the Florida Sporting Goods, my Uncle Howard enjoyed the position of president of the family business in West Virginia. Uncle Howard certainly fit the definition of success — driving a black Mercedes with its mahogany dash and black leather seats, at a time when Mercedes weren't so common, and spending weekends at his farm. I had thoughts about how I stacked up compared to these men.

In 1963, at age 30, I had returned home to Vero Beach, with a frazzled wife, three children under four, and a minor, but irritating, ulcer condition. We had been living in California and when Radiation, an electronics company in nearby Melbourne, Florida, agreed to maintain my salary of $10,000 per year and pay moving expenses, I was ready. However, to return home had not been my life's plan.

As a newlywed, five years earlier, I had more ambitious ideas. I remembered Katharine and I sitting on the stoop of our duplex on the Army post at Fort Huachuca, Arizona. In two weeks we would be packing up, and I would be leaving the Army so I could enter the University of Virginia's graduate business school. I remarked to Katharine half seriously, "Someday I'm going to be on the cover of *Business Week*."

"I suppose that will be when you become president of General Electric," she replied. I had been in a GE training program before going into the Army to fulfill my two-year ROTC commitment.

"Certainly," I said, smiling.

"Why not?" she agreed.

I looked at this girl in her plaid shorts and white knit shirt and thought, I'm a lucky fellow. We would soon go into our quarters furnished with one sofa, one table, and two chairs; get ready for bed; and hop into the two side-by-side army cots. Their steel-bar sides had been tied together per the suggestions of my Master Sargeant. With a double bedspread, received as a wedding present, stretched over both cots, our sleeping arrangements looked almost normal.

But things didn't turned out quite that way. Four years later, returning from a doctor's appointment one afternoon, Katharine and I walked into our house on Clarissa Lane in Tustin, California, paid the baby-sitter, and sent three-year-old Buck and two-year-old Mark out into the fenced-in back yard to play. Kit lay asleep in her crib. We went into the living room where we could keep an eye on the boys through the window. "Let's talk. You've got to talk," declared Katharine.

I hadn't said a thing driving home from the doctor. I had taken time off from Autonetics to hear the results of the tests and x-rays. Yes, I had an ulcer. It was small, but it was the reason why I had pain and tightness in the upper part of my stomach. I wished I could reach into my stomach and rip out the problem. And I had been short with Katharine the last few weeks. The doctor told me to stay home from work for a week, rest, sip Amphojel like my dad had done, eat cottage cheese which I disliked, drink plenty of milk, no beer, and take some pills that, he said, would relax me.

Was the ulcer caused by work? Probably. After all, as project manager for the target-loading equipment for the Minuteman Missile, I had been working 60 hours a week, and had had reviews with an uptight management who, at the time, were worried about faulty test missiles blowing up on the pad at Cape Canaveral. Anyway, I was one of 10,000 engineers and technicians working on the program just at Autonetics alone. Maybe my real problem was that I could never find my car in the parking lot if I went home at a decent hour, and I was scared every time I pulled out on the Southern California freeways.

"What's going on in that mind of yours?" asked Katharine. We had settled down on the couch. Out the window Buck was swinging on the play set; Mark was climbing the ladder to the slide. Our basset hound, Napoleon, sat on his haunches by the swing watching the boys. I didn't say anything for a minute. Katharine stared at me. She wasn't going to let me get away without talking this time.

"Am I going to be like Dad and have to quit work like he did? I'm thirty. He was about thirty when he moved to Florida. I can't quit work. I'd go crazy. We don't have any money; we have three kids. This ulcer thing has been in the family and now I've got it. Son-of-a-bitch," I blurted out. I felt tears surging into my eyes.

"Rody, wait a minute. Dr. Carlson said that with a week's rest, you'll probably be fine. You're not throwing up, you're not bleeding, you just have an ache in the stomach. They know a lot more about ulcers now than they did when your dad had it," she said.

She pushed her hand through her hair. "Go ahead and cry. It'd be the best thing you could do. You hold stuff in like your dad. You won't talk to me. Get mad! Scream! Throw something! If it's tough at work, come home and let it out. I'd rather you got it all out with one big bang rather than just pick, pick, pick at me like you've been doing. I don't need that. I've got my hands full with the kids."

So we left California and moved to Florida to escape the pressures of a job and a place that were giving me fits. In a way, I had followed in my dad's footsteps.

Dad gave us a lot in Kanawha Acres, the property where I had grown up. We built a house on two acres overlooking the lake, a far cry from the cul-de-sac in California. Instead of hitting a six-lane freeway every morning, I drove up U.S. 1 along the Indian River watching spectacular sunrises on my way to Melbourne and my new job.

Shortly after we had moved into our house, I received a call after dinner from my mom. "Rody, your dad is sitting in the bar at the Patio. There is something going on with the building. Maybe you ought to go down there and be with him."

The Patio sat right across the street from the Florida Sporting Goods. I walked in the back entrance of the dimly lit bar where a Beatles tune blared from the juke box, and saw Dad standing at the open door facing US-1 — gripping what I was sure was a bourbon and soda. He might have three drinks during the cocktail hour, but he never drank after dinner. I walked up to him.

"What's going on?"

"Look." He gestured across the street toward his building, glistening white in the glare from the streetlights. The Florida Sporting Goods name which once had spread the length of the building was now confined to a small arc over the west door. A car dealer's name dominated the rest of the building. Dad had gone from entrepreneur with a dream to landlord. Cars with their headlights on were rolling out of the building and being parked on the street.

"What the hell are they doing?" I asked.

"I called that bastard and told him if he didn't pay the rent, I was going to have the sheriff repossess the cars. They're moving them off the property. I guess he believed me about the sheriff," replied Dad.

"How far is he behind?"

"Three months. This sure isn't what I had in mind when I built the building. Let's go have a drink."

I followed him to the bar and we pulled up stools and sat down. We had the place to ourselves; the couple had left. The juke box was quiet. Dad lit a cigarette and then ordered another bourbon and soda; I had a Schlitz. We sat there drinking, not saying a word.

Finally, I said, "Pappy, I'm sorry."

"Not a damn thing we can do about it. Let's go home."

"You OK?"

"Yep." He put the half-empty drink down and got up.

We went out the back door and he climbed into his jeep and headed toward the beach. I watched him go and then went back into the Patio and finished my beer as all sorts of memories ran through my head.

The Florida Sporting Goods had been a good idea at the time, but now it was gone. It had given Dad a challenge after the frustrations of his Coast Guard duty. Did he look on it as a failure on his part, like his inability to handle the pressures of the family business when he was young?

But he had done some other things after the war, things he should have been proud of. When a piece of coal property had turned up in some old family records, Dad believed value still existed in the partially mined land, and he had the foresight to pay the back taxes. The coal royalties helped pay for college educations for my cousins and me.

When the Corps of Engineers decided to dredge a new channel for the Inland Coastal Waterway down the middle of the Indian River, Dad had his own ideas where it should go. He didn't want it to run through good fishing areas, or cause wakes from passing boats to hit the city docks, or make it difficult for boatmen to approach the drawbridge. He didn't want politicians making asinine decisions, so he ran for election to the Inland Waterway Commission. Unlike his competition, he didn't campaign in the local paper. He said, "People know me. If they want me, they'll vote for me." And they did.

After getting the channel properly placed, he resigned. He had accomplished his goal, and he wasn't going to stay around and deal with the political crowd. When a local contractor in the late '50s offered to convert the muck pond to a lake at Kanawha Acres, Dad decided to develop the property. That's when he had found the woolly mammoth and the saber-tooth tiger bones. Dad had maintained the natural beauty of the place by retaining the pines, the palms, the giant oak trees and an open area around the new lake. He had laid out one- and two-acre lots and had sold them to young couples who he thought truly appreciated the place, like Randy Sexton, who had had a tree fort on a corner of the property when he was a boy.

And for years Dad had been on the board of the family business, the Charleston Electric — traveling back and forth to West Virginia. When that business was sold and Uncle Howard retired, it had been Dad who had pushed to find a way to take care of the old-time employees, who had lost their jobs in the sale.

Within months after that evening at the Patio, the Florida Sporting Goods building no longer existed. Dad had sold it to an oil company, which tore it down and replaced it with a fancy service station.

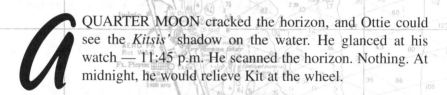

Chapter 12

Rescue
1942

A QUARTER MOON cracked the horizon, and Ottie could see the *Kitsis'* shadow on the water. He glanced at his watch — 11:45 p.m. He scanned the horizon. Nothing. At midnight, he would relieve Kit at the wheel.

In the *Java Arrow* engine room, Willard Hesse stood oiling the gigantic steam engine's crossheads, the roar of metal clanging against metal filling his ears, sweat pouring off his forehead. Suddenly a vibration rolled through the ship shaking Willard. An explosion like a thunderclap drowned out the engine room noise. "Jesus Christ, a torpedo!" he yelled.

Willard dropped his oil can with a clatter and moved as fast as he could to Philip Shera's position at the engine controls. "Let's get out of here!" he shouted at Shera.

"You go. I'm coming. Have to reverse the engine. The bridge telegraph says full astern. Can't launch the lifeboats with this kind of headway," Shera shouted back.

Willard ran for the ladder and climbed upward, arms and feet flying. As he reached the weather deck, another explosion came from below — the engine room. The concussion from the second torpedo flattened him. He heard Shera scream.

Pieces of metal ricocheted off the cabin walls above his head. The lights blinked, then went out, leaving the deck in darkness. Steam hissed from the fractured pipes below.

Dazed, Willard staggered to his feet and shook his head. His arm ached, but otherwise he felt OK. His only thought now was to get off the ship before she burst into flames.

The *Java Arrow* had four lifeboats, two alongside the aft deck house and two on the midships house. The crew had run drills while coming down the coast. Willard thought he should know what to do. He was closer to the stern. Go to the aft deck house, he told himself.

He moved toward the stern. Steam rose from the deck. He coughed as fumes penetrated his chest. There was no way he could head aft. Go forward, he thought.

He stumbled across the tank compartments as he ran toward midships. In the darkness he sensed, beyond the pounding of his feet, an eerie quietness. The thump, thump of the engine had ceased. The ship seemed to be losing headway. He saw no fire, smelled no smoke. The deck had a slight list to port, but seemed to have stabilized.

Reaching the midships house, Willard climbed to the second deck on the starboard side. The davits stood empty — the No. 1 lifeboat was gone. He looked over the side and saw it jammed with crew members, moving off from the ship. "They left me!"

He ran to the port side.

The No. 2 lifeboat had been lifted off the deck by the cranks. With the davits swung outward she hung suspended over the water, ready to be lowered. Men were lined up to go down a rope ladder that had been thrown over the side.

The lifeboat began to drop on its lines. As it flopped into the water with a splash, it righted itself quickly. The *Java Arrow*'s momentum had slowed to a creep, easing the impact. The lifeboat bobbed on the water, its side clanking against the tanker's hull. The crew climbed down the ladder and dropped into the boat. Willard climbed over the rail and grabbed the rope ladder. The rope pricked his hands; his feet tried to find the loops. Hand-over-hand he descended, as the ladder swung. His body scraped against

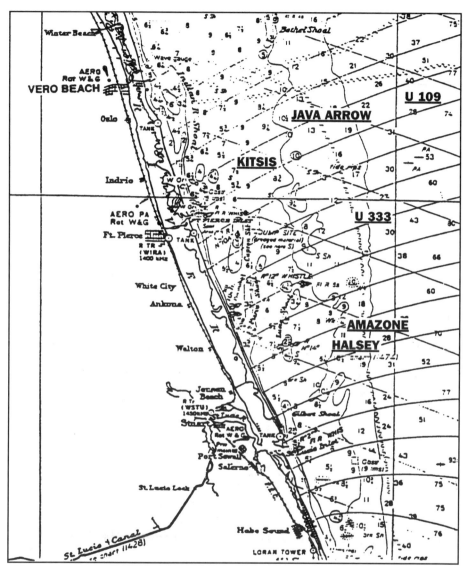

The location of the ships and boats involved in the attacks and rescue on the night of May 5-6, 1942, off the east coast of central Florida.

the metal hull. How much farther did he have to go? Was the ship going to explode? Then someone grabbed him and swung him into the lifeboat. He sat down with a thump, squeezed in between two other crewmen.

Sweeney stood in the bow, directing the operation. "Move forward. Tighten it up. This is all we've got," he yelled.

The tanker USS *Java Arrow* with a hole in her hull on the morning of May 6, 1942, after she was torpedoed by *U-333*.
The Mariners Museum, Newport News, VA

Captain Hennichen had arrived from the bridge and had followed Willard down the ladder, carrying a bag in the crook of his arm — the ship's codes and papers, thought Willard.

The Captain squeezed into the stern. He asked Sweeney, "What's the count? Have we got everybody?"

"Duggan has twenty-three in No. 1. Twenty-two in this one. We're short two. Stuart and Crawford made a final check. They couldn't get close to the engine room. Shera was on duty and he's not aboard the lifeboat," reported Sweeney.

Willard looked up, "He didn't make it, Mr. Sweeney. I was on duty with him. He told me to leave the engine room; he was shutting down the engine. I heard him scream."

"Jesus . . . ," Sweeney said. "Captain, are we ready to launch? This thing could still blow."

"Where is Mr. Fentress? Was he in the engine room?" asked Hennichen. No answer.

"OK let's shove off," ordered Hennichen.

Sweeney yelled at one of the crew sitting in the middle ahead of Willard. "Keep us away from the hull with your oar. Now get those oars set and start rowing. If the ship goes, we'll get sucked down with her!"

Willard was so squeezed in that he couldn't move. They must have had twice as many men in the boat as they should. No one was talking. The only noise was the squeak of the oars, the water lapping the ship's hull.

Willard looked up. The *Java Arrow* towered over the lifeboat. Slowly, they began to move away from the tanker as two of the crew rowed with the long oars. Even in the dark, Willard could see a giant gash in the hull rising from the water line. He nudged the guy next to him. "Look at that hole. If we had been carrying fuel in the bulk tanks, we would have been roasted."

Hennichen's voice came from the stern, "Let's go alongside the other lifeboat. Keep well off the ship. The engine room could go at any moment." The lifeboat moved forward. The tanker became a huge silhouette in front of the quarter moon low in the east. They circled the ship. Coming out from its lee, they began to roll with the southeast sea. Willard wondered if he was going to get seasick. He had never been that way on ships, even in big seas. Ahead he saw the other lifeboat. As they pulled alongside, hands reached out and grabbed the sides and held the two boats together. Hennichen had a conversation, which Willard couldn't hear, with someone in the other boat. Then Hennichen shouted in a voice that carried over both boats, "We're short two men. Shera was in the engine room when it exploded. Chief Engineer Fentress is missing. Did anyone see him?"

A voice from the No. 1 boat answered. "Captain, I saw Fentress heading down the companionway towards the engine room as I was getting out of the deck house. I don't know what happened to him."

Willard heard the Captain say, "Nothing we can do now."

The two boats sat side by side for a few minutes. The *Java Arrow* was slowly moving off, drifting with the sea.

Lanier said to Willard, "I wonder where that Nazi sub is. Probably looking at us through their periscope. They could surface and finish us off."

"Yeah," replied Willard. "She isn't sinking. They might put another torpedo in her. We need to get out of here."

Then he realized they were moving. Both boats were being rowed parallel to each other and now were a hundred yards from the ship.

A seaman sitting in front of Willard revealed, "I saw the sub after she torpedoed us. It was sitting on the surface. I've never been so scared in my life. I didn't know which way to go to the lifeboat."

"Did you tell somebody? Maybe the gunnery crew could have fired at it," asked Willard.

"No, those guys were in the lifeboat ahead of me."

Another voice said, "I heard one of the lookouts say that somebody had seen two subs out there."

"You men quiet down," cautioned Sweeney.

The two lifeboats sat side by side for a while as if nobody knew what to do. A swoosh came from the other boat as a flare rocketed into the sky, burst open, and spread a red glow over the boats and the distant hull of the *Java Arrow*. Willard ducked, putting his arm over his eyes, as if hiding from the light. He knew the sub was watching, and they were a target in the bright light of the flare. But nothing happened. They just sat rocking on the ocean. One of the men leaned over the side and vomited. Willard felt like he was ready to do the same. A half hour passed; someone launched another flare.

Aboard the *Kitsis,* Ottie stood at the wheel; he had relieved Kit. To the east-southeast he saw the darkness split by a red dot arcing skyward. It burst into a bright flash of light. Pointing, Kit yelled from the bow, "Flare!"

Ottie felt his heart beating. He held the boat steady as Kit came down from the bow and swung into the cockpit. Ottie stepped aside to let him take the wheel.

Harry bounced up from his chair. "What the hell is it?"

"A flare," said Ottie. In the distance, the light floated down toward the sea, swaying in the air beneath its small parachute.

Kit took the controls and advanced both handles. The engines roared. The boat kicked up a wake and surged forward. Toward the horizon, the flare winked out as it hit the water.

"How far, Ottie?" Kit asked.

"A couple of miles, hard to tell."

Ward stumbled into the cockpit from below. "What's going on?"

"A flare," explained Harry.

"From what?" asked Ward, rubbing his eyes.

"God only knows," said Kit, as he spun the wheel and turned the *Kitsis* toward the southeast. "Ottie, what time is it?"

"One forty-five."

Where were the rescue boats? The flares could certainly be seen from shore. Why hadn't they been picked up? Finally, Willard heard the Captain say, "We're going to put everybody who is hurt in the No. 2 boat with Sweeney; he'll take it to shore. Can't be more than seven to eight miles. No. 1 boat will stay here till someone picks us up. At some point we're going to have to put somebody back on board and get the anchor down. She's a menace to navigation."

It took several minutes to transfer the men. The Captain got into No. 1. Willard stayed where he was. His shoulder hurt; he felt like he would vomit at any moment. He didn't feel like crawling into the other boat. After the boats were reloaded, Sweeney directed the men at the oars in No. 2 to row toward the west. The quarter moon was slowly rising, but Willard could no longer see the *Java Arrow*.

As the lifeboat moved towards the coast, Willard lost track of time. Every once in a while he would hear the swoosh and see the red glow as

Sweeney launched another flare. His stomach felt better. He dozed. Suddenly he heard Sweeney shout, "There's some kind of boat ahead. Row towards it!"

Willard heard a motor above the sound of the oars hitting the water. He looked up and saw off the bow the dark outline of a small fishing boat.

With Kit running the *Kitsis*, Ottie had moved back on the bow. Ward and Harry stood in the stern. By now they had seen a series of flares, launched at 15-minute intervals. Kit continued to head in their direction at full throttle. The flash from each flare blinded Ottie, and he had trouble readjusting his eyes to the darkness of the ocean and the sky. Thoughts rolled through his head. Was it a disabled ship? Were survivors in the water? Were there lifeboats? Could it be the Germans who had fired the flare for some reason? All he knew was that they had to be getting closer.

Kit throttled the engine back. They moved into an area where it seemed they had last seen a flare launched. The quarter moon now glowed high in the eastern sky. Ottie saw a dark shape floating in the water. He pointed and yelled, "Kit, look off the port bow!"

"Yeah, I see it." He eased the *Kitsis* forward.

The form took shape. "Looks like a lifeboat. Put the spotlight on it," hollered Ottie.

Kit flicked on the spotlight. Ottie could see heads and shoulders crammed together from bow to stern. Some of the men in the boat threw up their arms to shield their eyes from the light. The boat sat low in the water, wallowing even in the small seas.

"God almighty, it's packed!" exclaimed Ottie. "We didn't see any ship hit. Where did they come from? Better turn off that light. Might be a sub out there."

"We can't tow 'em. They'll sink. We're going to have to take 'em on board," said Kit, turning off the spotlight.

"Yeah, where?" Ottie adjusted his eyes to the darkness.

"How many in that lifeboat, Ottie?"

"Close to twenty-five as best I can tell."

"Jesus!" Kit turned to Ward. "See if you can make room below. Some of those guys may be hurt." He edged the *Kitsis* toward the lifeboat.

Ottie came down from the bow and joined Harry in the cockpit. He took a line off the stern cleat and coiled it. When the lifeboat lay close enough, he hollered across the water, "I'm going to throw you a line. Grab it!"

A voice shouted back, "Throw it!"

Ottie swung his arm and tossed the coil. The line arced outward, straightened, and fell across the forward section of the boat. Several hands held it. He and Harry pulled the lifeboat alongside the *Kitsis* and tied her down. They helped the men over the side one by one and placed them in the boat. The men said little; a few mumbled thanks. They seemed in shock. Some had trouble walking, and Ottie discovered that their feet had been burned.

Harry and Ward carried a man down below and laid him on the bunk. Ottie guided those who seemed unhurt up onto the top of the cabin and told them to hang on to the handrail. Several men were below; most of the crew sat on the deck in the cockpit. Some wrapped themselves in blankets from the lifeboat. A couple of survivors had no more than sat down than they got up and vomited over the side. It was almost impossible for Ottie to move without stepping on a body.

The last man off the lifeboat turned to Ottie, "Name's Sweeney. Thanks."

"What happened?" Ottie asked.

"We were torpedoed, I guess, about three hours ago. We're off the tanker *Java Arrow*."

Ottie helped him to a spot on the cockpit floor by the transom. "Are there more survivors?"

"Yeah, there's another lifeboat with the Captain. It stayed with the ship."

"Find a place to sit. We'll take you guys into Fort Pierce. I'm sure the Coast Guard has seen the flares. They'll send a boat out for the rest of the crew," Ottie assured them.

Ottie checked his wristwatch. It was 3:45 a.m. He moved forward, stepping over and around bodies. He got to Kit who had stayed at the wheel, who was maneuvering the *Kitsis* to maintain minimum movement while the lifeboat was being unloaded. "What do you want to do with the lifeboat?" asked Ottie.

"Shove it off. We can't tow it. I'm not sure we're going to make it ourselves. We're carrying a hell of a load."

"Yeah, about twenty-five more than we should," agreed Ottie.

Ottie untied the line and gave the lifeboat a push as Kit edged the throttle forward. As the *Kitsis* crept ahead, the lifeboat disappeared off the stern into the darkness. Ward moved up on the bow to be with the eight or so men sitting there, while Harry leaned against the transom, watching the group sitting on the cockpit deck.

Ottie went below to check on the two men in the bunks and the two lying on the deck. One guy sat on the head. Ottie came back and stood next to Kit. "Everybody looks pretty settled," reported Ottie. "A guy below is in pain; I think he burned his feet. Some are puking, maybe from shock."

"Where did they come from? We sure didn't see an explosion," asked Kit.

"They're off a tanker — the *Java Arrow*. I think that's what the mate called her. They took two torpedoes. The mate said he thinks the ship stayed afloat. They could only launch two lifeboats. The Captain told this crew to head to shore. He stayed in the other lifeboat near the ship. They think two of the crew were killed."

"I hope we can get 'em in. We're sitting awful low."

"I'm sure glad there isn't much of a sea," remarked Ottie.

Willard sat on the cockpit deck, his back resting against the gunwale, his legs curled up under him. He felt better. The diesel engines vibrated under him. These fishermen, or whoever they were, seemed to know what they were doing. He was going to make it to shore.

During the next hour, the *Kitsis* crept slowly south toward the Fort Pierce Inlet. The quarter moon stood overhead. Many of the *Java Arrow* crew slept, heads on their arms, leaning against each other. Ottie and Kit stood side by side at the controls. Suddenly a flash lit the sea far to the southeast, then died back leaving a glow on the horizon.

"Son-of-a-bitch! That sub's got another one. What the hell is going on out here?" asked Ottie. The glow disappeared.

"Thank God we're getting near the inlet," declared Kit.

The *Kitsis* hit rough water at the mouth of the inlet. It was 5 a.m. A strong tide ran out between the two jetties, smacking into the small seas rolling in toward the beach. The boat's bow plowed into the turbulence and pushed against the force of the tide, bucking and swaying in the wave action. Ottie, standing in the cockpit, almost lost his balance. Kit, at the wheel, hollered to the crew on the bow to hang on.

The *Kitsis'* patrol report detailing the rescue of the *Java Arrow's* crew.

The cruiser cut through the rough water and then settled down. But Ottie noticed they were making slow headway against the tide. Then he saw water beginning to appear in the cockpit. Water was pouring in through the scuppers. The tanker crewmen sitting on the deck were getting wet, but they were so cramped they couldn't stand.

Ottie motioned to Kit and pointed to the water in the cockpit. Kit hollered, "Check the bilge!"

Ottie moved the crewmen out of the way and lifted the engine hatch. The roar of the engines and the smell of oil engulfed him. He saw that water had risen to the level of the engine block, flowing in from the cockpit. The bilge pump couldn't get rid of it fast enough. If it rose much higher, the engine would conk out. The exhaust pipe at the transom was already below water.

The consequences flashed through Ottie's head. Without power, the cruiser could drift back out the inlet broadside into the rough water. If they anchored, the bow would dig in, and they would take on even more water.

Ottie yelled at Ward to grab a couple of buckets sitting next to the transom. He dropped down into the bilge, his sneakers submerged in the oily water, and began bailing. He dipped and lifted the bucket to Ward who tossed the contents overboard. They worked furiously, like a fire brigade, aided by a couple of the tanker crewmen, but were hardly holding their own. The water sloshed back and forth in the bilge. The engine skipped a beat but kept running.

Ottie felt a tremor through the boat and fear flashed through him. Then he realized that Kit had brought the *Kitsis* safely alongside the Coast Guard Station dock.

Chapter 13

Riomar Beach
1942

Let's stop all this spreading of rumors. For weeks now the community has been flooded with rumors about this and that — mostly pertaining to . . . ship sinkings along the coast. . . . If we can't print it — you shouldn't discuss it. This is war time. All-out war, too.

Vero Beach Press Journal — May 15, 1942

J STOOD OUTSIDE the kitchen door in the warm early morning sunlight, a cigar box full of marbles in one hand and my book bag in the other, ready to head down the dirt road to the bus stop and to school. I was eight years old. I had said good bye to my mother; my father was not home yet. That was unusual since generally before leaving for school, I would peek into their bedroom and see him snoring quietly. Mom spoke in whispers while she fixed breakfast. She wouldn't say much about what he was doing other than he was out on the *Kitsis*, but I knew he wasn't fishing. He didn't fish every night.

Between marble games at school, I had heard talk of ships blowing up offshore and Nazi submarines. One kid said a window shattered in his house because of an explosion off the beach. I didn't believe him.

I heard the Model A, and my dad came rolling up the sandy driveway. The two bird-dogs romped out to greet him. Mom raced out of the kitchen past me, the screen door banging. As he got out of the car, she said frantically, "You're late. Is everything OK?"

Dad stood there in a dirty, stained T-shirt and damp dungarees. His dark hair, surrounding a coming bald spot, went in all directions; there had been no time for haircuts. At 35, with a prematurely receding hairline, he looked, my mom said, like the mad maestro. He had a short muscular build and a round, gentle face. I didn't know my father well then. My mother raised me and, as I think back on it, isolated me from my father to protect him from the confusion of having a child around.

Dad pulled a .22-caliber pistol in a black holster and a 12-gauge shotgun out of the car and laid them on the hood. I had asked before why he had the guns. He said he didn't like to leave them on the boat.

"We had a hell of a night. I'll tell you about it later," he said to Mom.

"Kit, are you all right?" she asked. I knew she meant his stomach.

"Fine. You know when I'm on the water I don't have any trouble."

He patted me on the shoulder, "Little man, you better head for school."

"Yes, sir." With my dog following, marbles in my cigar box rattling, I walked across the yard toward the path through the pines which led out to the road where the school bus stopped. I wondered what I wasn't being told. Was it dangerous what my dad did? He didn't act like it. But my mom seemed worried.

At mid-morning, Sis Johnson pulled her Studebaker up to the dock at the Fort Pierce Yacht Basin and parked opposite the *Kitsis*. She opened the car door and climbed out, grabbed a bucket of rags, Dutch Cleanser, and a mop from the back seat. She wore blue denim shorts cut off at the knees, a white blouse, and white sneakers. Kit had told her she was facing a mess, but she hadn't paid much attention. She was more concerned about him. He had looked so tired when he got home. She had stripped him of his wet, grubby clothes, sat him down at the kitchen table in his shorts, made him scrambled eggs, bacon and coffee, and then sent him upstairs to bed. At the same time, she had gotten Rody off to school. Kit had told her they had brought in a crew from a torpedoed tanker, nothing more. When he and Ottie had first started these patrols, she had been scared by all the stories about submarines offshore, but then Kit's trips had been routine, until now.

Sis gathered her cleaning equipment and walked over to the *Kitsis*. She pulled the spring line, moving the cruiser closer to the dock, and stepped on board. The stench of stale vomit engulfed her. She looked at the cockpit covered with a slime and streaks of blood. She wanted to heave. Could she do this? She had to.

Sis turned her face into the breeze coming off the Indian River, took a deep breath, and stepped down into the cockpit. Her sneakers hit the slime, and she slipped but grabbed the gunwale to keep from falling. Straightening up, she noticed a couple of gray blankets tossed over the fighting chairs. She didn't recognize them so she figured they must have been left by the tanker crew.

She climbed back on the dock, picked up a hose, and sprayed the cockpit, washing the gunk out the scuppers. When she had finished, she took another deep breath and climbed down into the cabin. She stripped the two bunks of their wet, blood-stained sheets. She scrubbed a blood spot out of one of the mattresses. She got down on her hands and knees and cleaned the head.

Finally, She felt like the *Kitsis* looked shipshape. She gathered up the wet bedding. She hesitated for a second as she looked at the gray blankets and then picked them up, too, and took them to her car. She was a mess herself. Her short hair lay stuck to her head, wet with perspiration; splotches smeared the front of her blouse, and her shoes would have to be scrubbed before she wore them again. As she turned the car around to head home, she took a quick look at the *Kitsis*, laying at its mooring in bright sunshine. "God, take care of Kit and Ottie," she prayed.

When I arrived home from school that day, Dad's car was gone, and Mom was coming in the driveway in the blue Studebaker. I waved and waited as she got out.

"Good day at school?" she asked, as she hugged me.

"Yes, ma'am. Where you been, Mom? You look . . . ," I hesitated.

"Dirty," she said, smiling. She patted her head, trying to straighten out her hair. "I've been in Fort Pierce cleaning up the boat."

"Is Dad fishing tonight?"

"Yes." The worried expression came back on her face. "You'll see him in the morning. Did you win any marbles today?"

"A couple," I answered.

The next morning Dad was asleep as usual when I left for school. When I came home, he was gone, but Mom was there.

"Your dad left you something, but you can't tell anybody at school. Promise?" We were in the kitchen. She picked up a short piece of board from a kitchen chair and handed it to me. It was a narrow wooden name plate, a couple of feet long, with letters cut into the gray painted wood. A bent screw hung out of one end, its threads sharp to the touch. At the other end, the paint was buckled as if it had been scorched.

I beamed with pleasure that my dad had given me this trophy. "What is it? What does it say?"

"*Amazone*. It's off a ship. Someday your dad will tell you the story."

"Can't you tell me, Mom?"

"Your dad hasn't really told me."

"Can I put it on my dresser?" I asked.

"Yes, Rody, but remember you must not talk about it," cautioned Mom.

"Yes, ma'am," I promised.

I ran upstairs to my room and placed the name plate on my dresser next to one of my prize possessions, a small wooden model of a PT boat. I stopped and looked at the board again. My dad had given it to me. It must be important.

Along with the name plate came four gray woolen blankets, wet and stained, some with blood. Mom had scrubbed them and hung them on the line in the back yard to dry. She said they had come from a ship too, but a different ship.

A few days after receiving the *Amazone* name plate, I went with my mother to the beach. I had pestered her to do this for some time, not so much to go swimming, but I thought I might see something on the ocean that would explain what Dad was doing. I had visions of masses of ships being chased by German submarines.

That Saturday morning, we piled into the Studebaker with beach towels and a rubber float to ride the waves. As we drove out the driveway, I waved at the men working on the observation tower that was going up between our house and the muck pond. It was as tall as the pine trees with steps leading to a platform with a shed on the top. It would be manned by volunteers 24 hours a day who would report, by telephone to Tampa, all airplanes flying overhead. Mom was rounding up the volunteers, mostly older people she knew, and she would run things while Dad was off on his patrols.

Driving out of the property, we crossed the bridge over a ditch that was the entrance to Kanawha Acres. Mom and Dad had named the place after the Kanawha River that runs through Charleston, West Virginia, where all our family still lived. Our two-story house sat on the dry part of 20 acres in a clearing surrounded by pines, oaks, and cabbage palms. The muck pond with tall grass, which I was sure held moccasins and alligators, covered the rest of the property. On this place, I romped and played cowboy with my dogs, chickens, and ducks. As the war progressed, I turned from cowboy to soldier, utilizing most of the property for maneuvers with my friends.

We lived three miles from town, and there wasn't much in between except cow pastures and orange groves. Downtown, Mom and I came to a halt at Vero's only stoplight. Here Route 30 (now State Road 60), which ran across the central part of the state west to Tampa, met Old Dixie Highway, a two-lane road running the length of Florida's east coast from Jacksonville to Miami.

At the corner across from the post office, we pulled into Horace Gifford's filling station. Mr. Gifford was a friend of my dad's. He asked how Kit was doing. He only saw him coming and going to Fort Pierce.

"He's tired but doing all right," Mom told him.

"He's wanted me to go with him a couple of times, but with kids going into the service I have trouble finding help and can't get away. I know Ottie's been going with him pretty regular. I hear some strange things are going on out there." He turned to ask me about my ducks.

"They're fine, Mr. Gifford," I replied.

Mom asked Horace to fill up the gas tank while she ran across the street to the post office.

"Can I go down the street and see what's playing at the movie?" I asked.

Saturday afternoon movies were an institution for the kids in Vero. I had been allowed to go occasionally with my friend Ronnie. For nine cents we could see a double feature, a serial, and the news — London under bombardment; U.S. ships in the Pacific. A movie starring Gene Autry was playing that day. I didn't like him; he sang and was too sissified.

When I got back to the car, Mom wasn't there. I knew she would be talking with someone. Vero was small; you knew everybody in town. Finally she appeared. "Who did you see in the post office?" I asked.

"Mrs. Hardee. She said Dr. Hardee's brother is missing in the Pacific."

"Oh," I said. "Does that mean he's dead?"

"No, sometimes in war they can't find people. They don't know whether they are alive or dead," she explained.

Mom quickly pulled a letter out of her purse. "We received a note from Aunt Pye. It's from Williamsburg, Virginia."

She opened the letter and read it to herself and then looked up. "Uncle Howard has been made an officer in the Navy and is in minesweeper school. They're living in the Williamsburg Inn and your Cousin Ann is with them."

I asked if my dad was in the Navy.

"No, Rody. He's a volunteer in the Coast Guard Auxiliary," Mom answered.

"Will he go in the Navy?"

"He'd like to, that or the Coast Guard, but with his ulcer I don't think they'll take him," she explained.

"Why not? He goes out in the ocean every night," I persisted.

"I know, but that's different. They have funny rules," Mom said.

I liked my Uncle Howard, Dad's twin brother. When he and Aunt Pye visited, he would kid me — asking if I wanted to wrestle and making funny motions as if he was going to pin me. He had been a wrestling champion at Cornell as well as a quarterback on the football team. My dad hadn't gone to college. He didn't even seem to go to work like my friends' fathers, who sold cars or worked in the drugstore or owned a clothing store. I wasn't sure what he had done before the war had started.

We left Mr. Gifford's gas station, then waited at the railroad crossing as the Florida East Coast Champion pulled into the depot. Heading toward the beach, we passed the Royal Park Inn, now closed for the season, and the Episcopal Church where on Sundays my great-uncle George, a retired minister, sat in the front pew. We drove past the golf course and down the road lined with tall palms until we came to the Indian River. We rattled across the wooden bridge, feeling the jar from every wooden crossbeam. The bridge stretched almost half a mile just a few feet above the water. Up the river, I could see the small islands with tall Australian pines and the tin roof on the building at the city dock where Dad kept the *Kitsis*, when it wasn't in Fort Pierce.

I waved at Mr. Woods, the one-armed bridge tender. He and his family lived in a house built as part of the bridge on pilings beside the draw. He waved back with the stub of his arm that ended at the elbow. Whenever a boat approached, he inserted a metal tee in the draw and leaned on it while walking in a circle, slowly cranking it open. People usually got out of their cars to watch the boats pass through. Then Mr. Woods would crank the draw closed.

Across the bridge, we entered a tunnel of trees and could see the beach, a bright circle of light ahead. At the Beachland Hotel, we turned south past the Sunny Surf Cottages, the Driftwood Inn, the city beach with its thatched roof picnic pavilions, and a pink stucco, Spanish-looking house right on the water's edge. We were now in Riomar, with its winter houses boarded up for the summer.

Mom parked at the Riomar Beach Club, and we walked through its breezeway to the sand beyond. Across the unpaved shell road stood the Corner Cottage that we had rented for a couple of winters, before we had built the house west of town.

We walked down the steps of the beach club, and I dashed out on the sand to see the great battle taking place on the ocean. The horizon lay empty, the ocean peaceful, sparkling in the morning sun — no ships burning on the sea, no great convoys, no German submarines with periscopes cutting through the water. Small waves lapped the sand; a slight breeze flowed in from the southeast. Only the boiler lay out there, a quarter-mile offshore to the northeast, and I knew about it — a leftover from the ship *Breckinridge* which ran on a reef in the late 1800s. What was my daddy doing offshore every night, anyway?

Overcoming my disappointment with the peaceful sea, I walked with Mom across the hot sand to lay down our towels. My mom had taken off her jacket and looked young in her yellow one-piece bathing suit. At 28 she was sometimes taken for my sister.

I raced to the water's edge and stopped short. I pointed at the small waves. Dark filmy streaks laced the surface. A residue of gummy black material lay along the sand. I called back over my shoulder, "What's that stuff in the water, Mom? Ugh!"

"It looks like tar or oil, Rody," said Mom, as she caught up with me.

"Where did it come from?"

"I don't know. It's sure a mess. Don't go in the water. You'll get it all over you."

"Is it from the *Amazone*?" I asked.

Mom hesitated. "It could be, I suppose. Let's walk; we can't swim today."

We headed south down the beach toward the cove where the Riomar Golf Course ran right alongside the ocean. Black streaks ran through the water. Dark patches floated on the surface. As we walked, we passed scattered boards and trash. Farther on, several oil barrels rolled slowly back and forth in the surf. A gray life preserver, with the cloth ripped, part of the flotation material showing, rested on the sand just beyond the high-tide line of seaweed. I started to go pick it up. Grabbing my hand, Mom suggested we go home.

Were dead sailors in the water? I wanted to see more. "Ah, Mom, we just got here."

"We're going home, Rody."

Chapter 14

Fathers
1989

*T*HE EVENING after my chat with Peter in his back yard, he and Marc were my guests for dinner. Earlier, I had asked Peter if he and his wife would join me.

Peter hesitated. "My wife cannot come. Might we take Marc instead?"

"Certainly," I answered.

I had sensed all afternoon that in addition to Marc there was someone else in the house. Yet, Peter had made no mention of his wife, and her absence seemed peculiar. She had not been present either when Marilynn had visited Peter and his daughter at their North Sea cottage. Later as we drove to dinner, Peter said, with almost an apologetic smile, "My wife prepared some sweets and tea for us this afternoon, but I had already taken you back to the hotel."

Returning to the inn in the Bismarck Forest, Marc, Peter, and I were ushered into the candlelit dining room and shown a table by Peter's friend, the innkeeper. Father and son selected side-by-side chairs. I sat across from them.

I looked at Peter as he settled into his chair. He was dressed in a blue blazer, a white shirt with blue stripes, and a blue tie with lions' heads — the English lion, he had explained. In coat and tie, Peter's similarities to Uncle Howard seemed even stronger than when I had noticed them the day before. Marc too wore a coat and tie. His clean-cut looks, I couldn't help thinking, reminded me of the close-ups of the handsome young people of the German youth movement who had appeared in newsreels during the war.

We began dinner with a white wine, melon, and duck, followed by sea devil from the Mediterranean. I asked Peter what a sea devil was. He explained that I would know it as manta ray and that the bones were the "devil" part. As we talked, I felt a camaraderie between father and son. When Peter spoke, Marc would stop eating and listen to him attentively. To anyone glancing at the table they would seem to be grandfather and grandson.

While we sipped red wine and worked on the main course of venison, per the menu "fresh from the forest," we discussed Marc's education. As a student at the University of Bonn, preparing for a career in the foreign service, he had been taught little about World War II; German history was limited to the last 40 years, starting with the postwar German Republic. The conversation sounded similar to the one I had had with the blond on the flight over. Peter went on to say that Germans are discouraged from going into the war archives even though foreigners are given free access.

Peter excused himself to go to the men's room, and in the course of the conversation with Marc, I asked about his relationship with his father, "Is your father a bit rigid?"

He smiled shyly. "Partly," he answered.

When Peter returned to the table, the waiter had served a dessert of strawberries and cream, and Marc was talking about his sister Audrey, saying that she was a good runner and sometimes competed in marathons. Peter told about when Audrey had been in elementary school, and one of her classmates had raised a hand and said "Heil Hitler" to her. This had resulted from a photograph in the German newspapers showing Peter holding the plaque at Admiral Doenitz's funeral. Audrey had come to the United States as an exchange student in high school and later returned to attend the University of Wisconsin.

"Once there," Peter remarked, "they do not return. I do not understand her expressions when we talk on the telephone." There was a sadness in his eyes.

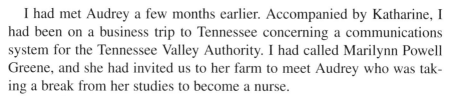

I had met Audrey a few months earlier. Accompanied by Katharine, I had been on a business trip to Tennessee concerning a communications system for the Tennessee Valley Authority. I had called Marilynn Powell Greene, and she had invited us to her farm to meet Audrey who was taking a break from her studies to become a nurse.

We arrived on an Indian Summer day. The trees on the rolling hills were at the peak of their fall colors. Audrey greeted us in shorts, barefoot, and holding a baby kitten in the palm of her hands — obviously very much at home on this Tennessee farm. I did not think of Audrey as pretty, but she had a striking face. Marilynn came up from the pasture and joined us. We talked about Peter. I said I hoped to meet him sometime. In our telephone conversations and his letters, Peter had never mentioned his wife so I asked Audrey about her mother. She took a snapshot out of her wallet. We saw the profile of a dancer in leotards — she had features like the movie actress Leslie Caron. Katharine looked up at Audrey and said, "She's beautiful." I nodded.

"She teaches ballet and jazz in Hamburg," explained Audrey. "She has cystic fibrosis. I don't know how she does it, but I've been in her classes, and I can't keep up with her."

Her mother's disease, I learned, occurs in the lungs and affects food digestion and breathing.

I asked Audrey how old her father was.

"He doesn't like to talk about it," She said, smiling. "My mother and father fell in love on a sailboat. He told her he was ten years younger than he really was. He didn't tell her his true age until just before they were married."

I mentioned to Audrey a story or two about Peter during the war that I had found during my research. She had not heard them and replied, "My father didn't tell me about those things. He talked to my brother, who is more interested."

Marc, Peter, and I finished our dinner, I paid the bill, and they dropped me by the hotel. I wasn't sleepy, so I stopped in the empty bar and had a beer. I wondered what kind of father Peter had been to Marc and Audrey.

He obviously had a busy career, and when they were children, growing up, he had been in his 60s, old enough to be their grandfather. Did he take them to soccer games and teach them to sail? Sipping my beer, I couldn't remember my dad and I doing much together when I was a little boy. Then I thought about the time I had accompanied him to the Coast Guard Auxiliary meeting.

It was 1945 — the Germans had surrendered, and the atomic bomb had been dropped on Japan. One afternoon Dad said to me, "Rody, there's a Coast Guard meeting tonight at the high school. The brass is coming up from Miami; I'm supposed to be there. Would you like to go?"

I beamed. "Yes, sir." I had just turned 12.

I sat beside Dad in a classroom, looking at two uniformed Coast Guard officers who stood up front by the teacher's desk with Uncle Press, my dad's friend, the town's Coast Guard Auxiliary Commander. Also in the room were Ottie Roach and maybe 15 other men.

The senior officer, decked out in his tan uniform and the stripes of a Lieutenant Commander, went on and on about how proud the Coast Guard was of the service performed by this unit — the rescue of crewmen from the sinking ships, the bravery of the volunteers going offshore every night, and how all this had helped win the war. I figured this officer had not been around in 1942 when the real action had taken place. Dad had mentioned that he gave the same speech at every little town on the Florida coast with an Auxiliary unit. But as far as I was concerned he was talking about my dad and *only* my dad.

I looked at my father with pride. I was waiting for him to be called forward to receive his medal. Uncle Howard had received two medals, the Silver Star and the Bronze Star. Aunt Pye had sent a copy of the citations for us to read. He had received the Silver Star after he had led a minesweeping unit during the landings at the Anzio beachhead in Italy in January 1944. It read: "Lieutenant Johnson handled his ship skillfully and with flawless determination throughout the execution of hazardous minesweeping operations to clear approach channels for the passage of assault boats and fire support areas off the hostile shore. This occurred despite constant enemy aerial attack, shellfire in the shipping areas, and adverse weather."

The Bronze Star had come for his "meritorious achievement as a minesweeper Section Commander during the amphibious invasion of Southern France in August 1944. He had directed the sweeping of enemy mines in the Bay of Toulon clearing a safe approach that had allowed the Allied Forces the facilities of a major port at which supplies and reinforcements could be landed in volume to support the ground movement northward into enemy-held territory."

The citations were sprinkled with words like: "fearless," "gallantry," "extreme efficiency," "courageous," "inspiring leadership," "exceptional ability," "cool and deliberate action," and "outstanding devotion to duty." Uncle Howard was a hero.

My dad didn't receive a medal in that classroom, but Certificates of Appreciation were given to each man. When my father stood up to receive his, I was pleased and proud. The evening concluded with the awarding of small brass plaques to those yachtsmen and fishermen, who had donated their boats to the Coast Guard for the duration of the war.

By August 1942, the Navy and the Coast Guard had enough ships and boats available, and volunteers were no longer needed offshore. Dad had given the *Kitsis* to the Coast Guard. In receiving her, the government judged her condition as fair and valued her at $4,500, plus equipment on board worth $250. The galley list included: a tea strainer, an egg turner, a lemon squeezer, 11 dinner plates, and 11 teaspoons. The shot glasses and bourbon had been removed. The balance of the ship's inventory indicated a well-equipped vessel. And so, my father's "pride and joy" as my mother called her, headed to war to be used by a bunch of Coast Guard draftees, most of whom had never set foot on a boat.

And my father followed the *Kitsis* by joining the regular U.S. Coast Guard as a Chief Petty Officer. Somehow, the Coast Guard doctors had closed their eyes, my Mom said, and ignored Dad's stomach condition. Perhaps, some higher rank had passed the word: The Coast Guard needed men experienced at sea who knew the Florida coastline. Besides, this man had an outstanding record in the Coast Guard Auxiliary.

Without any college, Dad was not eligible for officer's rank like Uncle Howard. Chiefs, like Army Master Sergeants, were the experienced 20-year men who had worked their way up through the ranks. I think Dad was more pleased being a Chief than an officer. Lots of men who didn't know one end of a boat from another became Navy and Coast Guard officers — not true of Chiefs. The rank didn't come easy; my dad had to pass a bunch of tests.

A friend of Dad's, home on leave, taught him how to march and do drill routines with a rifle. I stood on the edge of the yard thinking my father looked silly parading around in his dungarees and tee shirt, his shotgun on his shoulder with a man in an Army uniform hollering commands at him, "Forward march. To the rear march. Right shoulder arms."

I knew my father hated this, thought it silly. He wasn't much for regimentation. Our two bird-dogs chained to an oak tree at the edge of the yard lay in the dirt whining. They didn't seem to understand this marching any better than I did. Why would anyone have to teach my dad how to carry a gun? He had hunted and lived with a gun all his life. In my mind, no one knew more about the ocean and guns than he did.

At night, I heard the "da-da-dit" from the den as he practiced Morse Code with my mother. He taught me how to type out an S-O-S. The little light on the battery-operated machine flashed with each stroke of the key. Finally, he took the tests, passed, and was sworn into the Coast Guard in Miami.

From an old, converted houseboat, the *YHB-22*, Dad ran a group of small boats like the *Kitsis* that conducted patrols along the Florida West Coast. Most of his crew were recruits who had never been on the water. And there was no action. The U-boats had moved from U.S. waters out into the Atlantic to attack convoys. The last straw for Dad was when they had his crew paint the Sanibel Island lighthouse. His stomach condition, which had been overlooked when he had joined two years earlier, became the basis for a medical discharge. My mother had remarked, "Your father was the only person ever to get a discharge for an inability to eat onions."

In that high school classroom, Dad stepped forward to receive a brass plaque inscribed to the *Kitsis*. He brought it back to his seat and handed it to me. I thought it wonderful, but knew it would never be mounted on the cruiser. She had already been returned, and Dad had sold her for junk. She had been beaten to death for three years by men who knew nothing of the sea or boats. He had plans to build *Kitsis IV* in a boat yard in Fort Pierce.

We drove home in silence. I was shy, and Dad didn't express his thoughts. But I knew something was going on in his mind. He certainly hadn't expected anything special for what he had done in the war, but he did resent the treatment of his boat. As for those windbags and their fancy speeches, his attitude was "forget 'em."

Kit Johnson as a Chief Petty Officer in the U.S. Coast Guard, after the rescue of the USS *Java Arrow* crew and his other night patrols as a member of the Coast Guard Auxiliary.

From that point on, Dad and I began to spend time together. He thought I should learn to hunt. My father, Mr. Gifford, and three of his other friends leased 5,000 acres west of Vero Beach. The property contained scrub pines and palmetto with a few Brahma cattle scattered about — perfect country for quail, an occasional deer, and sometimes a flock of turkeys. This camp was the means through which my father entered my life. I was now considered old enough to handle a shotgun. I weighed less than a hundred pounds and was about as thin as the 410 he gave me. Before I was allowed to put a shell in the breach, he drilled me in safety in the back yard, much in the manner he had learned to march before going into the Coast Guard. I carried the weapon empty to prove that I could keep the barrel toward the ground, that in excitement I would not point it at someone. After I had proven myself, I was allowed to hunt with the men.

We used jeeps to hunt quail with Dad leading the way. He drove; I stood in the back. The dogs, setters and pointers, ranged ahead of us. When one went on point, we stopped, got off the jeep, loaded the guns, and walked up behind the dogs, their tails extended and quivering. Waiting for the air to explode as the covey flushed, I too quivered.

When the birds rose in a cloud of whirring wings, the challenge was to pick one, pull through its flight trajectory, and press the trigger, then do the same thing on a second bird before all were out of range. I had difficulty with this.

My dad instructed, "Rody, you're just throwing up the gun and firing. You have to pick out one bird." That advice was a lesson on life.

Dad kept tight control on the hunting. If four or five birds were shot out of a covey, he wouldn't allow anyone to go after singles, and since the coveys stayed in set areas, we wouldn't hunt that area the rest of the season. I saw my dad as the quiet leader of these hunting expeditions. I also saw a trait he very rarely displayed: intolerance — applied to anyone he considered a game hog or careless with a gun. He wouldn't hunt with those kind of men.

The hunting property was appropriately named Camp Imperial. The name came from a cheap bourbon whiskey that was the hunters' prime drink at the campsite. But when it came time to hunt, the Imperial stayed behind. At the end of the day, everyone returned to the elegant lean-to with a tin roof, placed under the spreading branches of a huge oak. Twelve could sleep side by side on air mattresses on the wooden floor.

All the cooking, presided over by Mr. Gifford, was done outside on a Coleman stove. The food ranged from venison, wild turkey, wild boar, and tough steak from range cattle to armadillo, raccoon, and rabbit, thrown in a big pot and cooked for hours.

The dogs lay in the shadows until the cooking smells got too much, and then they'd try to sneak into camp. They would be greeted by a thrown boot. An especially good hunting dog might be allowed to sleep next to his master under the lean-to, but that was the exception.

The camp talk concentrated on the day's hunting — who missed the easiest shot, whose dog pointed an armadillo instead of a quail, and arguments over who killed what bird when two shots were fired simultaneously.

In this atmosphere I was weaned from my mother and entered a man's world. And yet, she frequently hunted with us, the only woman to do so. She had always hunted with my father, shot well, and was considered a good sport by my father's friends.

After the weekend's hunting, my father and I would put the dogs in the back of the jeep, load our gear, and drive the 20 miles home — lights piercing the dark dirt roads, wind blowing in the sides of the jeep. We would ride in silence, comfortable in our closeness and the day we had shared. Dad might compliment me. "That was a good shot this morning, Rody."

Hunting with my father went on for several years until girls and parties became a higher priority, but the experience had been implanted and like playing football or the first girlfriend, it was part of my being.

As I sat in the hotel in Reinbek drinking a beer, I thought about Uncle Howard as a father and how he and Peter might be similar. As a teenager I had spent a couple of summers working in the family business, living with him and Aunt Pye. And with two daughters, they treated me like a son. Like Peter, Howard was a stickler for tradition, always insisting on a coat and tie for dinner, and there were constant reminders about table manners.

In his way, Uncle Howard helped me grow up. He would needle me about getting a haircut, shining my shoes, or if he thought I was goofing off while helping him with the yard work. When I fed his bird-dogs, I always had the food either too wet or too dry. This was the uncle who once, when we were on a trip, wouldn't stop the car and let me relieve myself. "Hold it," he told me. "Use some self control. Be tough."

And when we were hunting and both shot simultaneously at the same grouse, he claimed the bird as his. It would have been my first grouse. A picture of the event showed us each holding a leg of the grouse in a mock tug of war. Of course, he always had a twinkle in his eye and a slight smile as he put me through these exercises. But I never felt I could quite satisfy him.

It wasn't that way with Dad. And yet, I loved my Uncle Howard, because I knew he cared for me. He certainly seemed more like the successful fathers of my friends in boarding school and college. I was always a little surprised when I brought those friends home to visit and they really took to my dad.

Fishing gave Dad and me the same companionship as hunting. I thought about the time Dad and I had gone tarpon fishing in the Thousand Islands at the tip of the Florida peninsula. It was the summer after my junior year in high school. We were drifting in a 15-foot aluminum boat at the mouth of the Shark River, one of many rivers and creeks that cut through the mangroves and flow out of the Everglades into Florida Bay and the Gulf of Mexico.

Tarpon rolled all around, breaking the water with their backs and fins. We cast frantically, waiting for a hook-up. Finally, one struck Dad's Heddon top-water plug like an explosion, cleared the surface a couple of times with leaping jumps, and then headed for deep water and the open sea. The fish looked to be 75 pounds, and on Dad's light service reel would present a battle. Dad moved forward in the small boat, and directed, "Fire up the outboard, Little Man! We're going to have to chase this fellow."

I cranked the motor a couple of times, worrying that maybe I couldn't get it started.

Dad, standing at the bow, turned and yelled, "Come on! Let's get going."

Meanwhile, line was zinging off his reel. I was nervous about failing in a critical situation. Finally, the motor fired.

"That's a boy!" he shouted.

I headed the boat out the mouth of the creek into open water. Our typical roles had reversed. I was running the boat; he was fishing. All of a sudden, I was the Captain. Once we were out of the lee of the mangroves, small waves kicked up bouncing the boat.

The fish ran. Dad balanced himself, holding the rod high, then pumping to retrieve line. The tarpon cleared the surface, flashed its silver side in the sun, smacked the water, and went deep. Dad hung on, though I could see sweat on his face.

Spray from the bow spanking through the waves showered me. We were taking on some water. Using one hand to steer, I bailed with the other, using a rusty coffee can. We plowed on. I lost track of time. I could see the strain on the bent rod, Dad's arm muscles tight as he gripped the reel.

Then all went quiet, except the splashing of water against the sides of the boat. The bow swung and we began rolling in the sea. It took a second for me to realize that the outboard had quit. I was paralyzed; I didn't know what to do.

Dad hollered, "Rody, grab that can and put some gas in the motor. Quick!"

We were rocking, now some two miles offshore. I knew Dad had been keeping an eye on some thunderheads building to the west out in the Gulf. The reel whined as the tarpon ran with the line. I balanced myself and tried to pour gas into the motor. More spilled into the bottom of the boat than into the small tank, but finally it filled to the top and ran over. I cranked the motor a couple of times, worried that it wouldn't start. Finally it fired, and we were on our way again. Dad took his eyes off the line cutting through the water, turned to me, and said, "Good man!"

We kept following the tarpon who seemed determined to head for Mexico. I began to wonder if we might not have to let him go and head back to shore. I figured Dad was thinking the same thing. Suddenly the rod snapped straight; the line fluttered.

Dad explained, "Son-of-a-bitch!" and shrugged his shoulders. "Let's go home."

I turned the boat toward shore, disappointed that we had failed, but proud that we had fought the battle together, and that I, for the first time, had been running the boat.

In the hotel in Reinbek, I took the last swallow of beer, placed the bottle on the bar, said good night to the bartender, and headed upstairs to bed.

Chapter 15

German Naval Memorial 1989

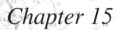

*T*HE NEXT MORNING, a Sunday, Peter picked me up for a trip to the Naval Memorial at Laboe on the Baltic Sea, north of Kiel. There the German navy had placed a U-boat as part of the memorial, and I was excited by the idea of touring it with Peter. Driving through Hamburg, we seemed thwarted at every street by a mammoth marathon being run through the city. Peter mumbled under his breath at each stop as he maneuvered through the streets trying to get beyond the runners' path. At an intersection where we were stopped, he ran a hand through his thin hair and exclaimed, "On Sunday, it should be easy to cross the city, but not today. It is like driving from Reinbek to my office every day, very difficult."

I felt Peter's frustration showed his age rather than the traffic situation.

At a hotel near the Hamburg airport, we picked up two American business associates of Peter's. Both were from Sperry Marine in the U.S., one an engineer in his 40s, the other a young marketing fellow. The engineer shook Peter's hand earnestly as he got in the front seat;

the younger man greeted, "Hi, Peter," and squeezed in the back seat with me. We left the city and zoomed through the country on the autobahn. All of us being in the electronic systems business, we had much to chat about.

An hour later, approaching the memorial, we saw a tall tower — the top like the bridge of a submarine. It stood at the head of Kiel Bay near the entrance of the Kiel Canal, which provides a shipping lane from the Baltic Sea to the North Sea and on to the Atlantic Ocean.

"Merchant and naval ships dip their flags as they pass in honor of all those who died at sea," said Peter, proudly.

We parked and immediately headed for the U-boat, a Type-VII similar to *U-333*. It sat below the tower on the beach like a giant model on a stand. Around its hull families played on the sand, braving the brisk breeze off the Baltic to enjoy the bright sun. Wind surfers skipped across the white-caps on the bay. Beyond, ship traffic moved in and out of Kiel.

To see a real U-boat was a thrill for me, and I was impatient while we stood in line for our inspection tour to begin. We entered through the stern at the engine room. To the rear was the aft torpedo tube.

Peter, pointing to the deck, said, "Here is where we stored an extra tor-pedo for the Florida mission."

With Peter leading the way we proceeded forward lifting our legs, bending from the waist, and twisting our bodies, to step through bulkhead doors as we advanced compartment by compartment. In the control room he pointed out and briefly explained the gauges, push buttons, wheels, switches, tubes, and pipes, but I had difficulty comprehending it all. The periscope shaft split the room, protruding downward from the conning tower through a slot in the deck and into a casing in the hull. Peter stopped and sat down on a stool. As he pointed to a ladder, he told us that the periscopes, engine room repeater, and torpedo firing lever were located in the conning tower.

"When we submerged rapidly, I was washed down into the conning tower from the bridge," he said, with a quick smile.

He kept talking, but he looked tired in the glare of a naked light bulb — his face lined, bags under his eyes, the skin from his cheeks hanging loose-ly. I suddenly realized that he was an old man and that a lifetime had passed since he, the "Baby Sailor" in the Paris restaurant at the height of youthful bravado, had commanded a submarine. On this day in this sub-marine, he might have already had the cancer that would kill him three years later.

Peter Cremer (l) with Rody Johnson in front of a U-boat display at the German Naval Memorial at Laboe, on the Baltic Sea, north of Kiel, 1989.

He rose from the stool and gamely led us through the next bulkhead into an area that contained the commander's quarters. To me it looked like a small closet.

Peter explained, "I could lie in this bunk, listen to the sounds, feel the vibrations, and tell the condition of my boat."

We moved forward through more compartments, stopping at the bow torpedo room and crew's quarters. The compartment seemed packed with bunks. Peter described how 24 men slept there — 12 per shift, in what he called "the hot sack" routine. The new shift would get up, and the old shift would crawl in the just-emptied bunks.

We climbed out of the tight confinement of the U-boat hull and into bright sunshine and the crisp breeze. I took a gulp of fresh air and stretched my legs. Fifty-five people in that thing for ten weeks, crossing the Atlantic and back — I couldn't imagine it! A half-hour had been enough for me.

Leaving the U-boat, we walked up the hill to the memorial and entered the Hall of Honor, a barren room with cement walls painted with hundreds of ship silhouettes and swastikas on the walls, each one representing a sunken ship or submarine from both World War I and II. On the cold concrete floors, adding to the despair of the place, lay an occasional withered bouquet left in memory of someone lost at sea. I was struck by the futility of what the Germans had done in starting World War II and that Peter had been a hero in such an endeavor.

I remembered the numbers of U-boat crewmen killed — 30,000 of the 40,000 men that had served. Peter had miraculously escaped being part of those statistics, considering he had been at sea on *U-333* from 1941 to 1944. But then, 6,000 U.S. Merchant Mariners had lost their lives primarily because of the U-boats. That, of course, included Shera and Fentress on the USS *Java Arrow*. Fourteen Dutch crewmen had been lost at sea as the SS *Amazone* burst into flames and sank immediately after being torpedoed by *U-333*. And it was only by a miracle that the crew of the USS *Halsey*, loaded with oil, had survived. I didn't know the death toll for a British ship sunk in mid-ocean by *U-333* on its way home from Florida, but it could have been the whole crew.

Peter had been talkative at the beginning of the U-boat tour; in the memorial he was quiet. I walked outside and despite the sunshine was depressed by the feeling that I had visited a memorial to death. And for what?

On the trip back to Hamburg, I sat crunched in the rear seat of Peter's Mercedes coupe with the younger of Peter's business acquaintances. In a low voice, he made disparaging remarks.

"My God, he drives fast. Do you think he can see that well?"

"I think he drives damn well. He's had a long day, chauffeuring us about," I replied.

Later, as we had stopped at a light before getting on the autobahn near Kiel, there was another comment, "Should I say something to him about getting his brakes fixed?" I ignored his comment, though the brakes did sound pretty bad when he stopped at intersections.

About halfway to Hamburg this fellow fired off another one, "I have some respect for this old guy now that I've read his book. You know that he reports to our Copenhagen office, but, since he is in marketing, he really works for me."

I had had enough and didn't speak the rest of the way.

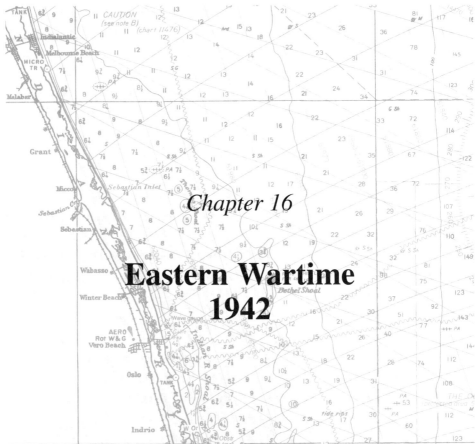

Chapter 16

Eastern Wartime 1942

*A*FTER THE ATTACK on the *Java Arrow*, Peter Cremer moved *U-333* a few miles to the south. He wanted to escape any Coast Guard or Navy ships, if they indeed existed, rushing to the tanker's rescue. Selecting a spot off the Fort Pierce Inlet, he positioned his boat so as again to silhouette ship traffic against the bright shoreline. With a tanker to his credit he felt a quiet satisfaction. The sub's luck had turned after the engine breakdown in mid-Atlantic and the ramming by the British tanker. He had proven that his boat could successfully attack despite its limitations.

Cremer put *U-333* on the bottom in 30 feet of water and took a rest, knowing that he could not stay on his feet 24 hours a day. He must pace himself, to be ready physically and mentally for the next attack. Turning the boat over to his Number One, he removed his cap and lay down on his bunk. Tuned to the vibrations of his boat, he slept lightly.

At 3:15 a.m., beeps from the sound room announcing an approaching ship woke Cremer. He jumped up, went to the control room, took over from his Number One, called the crew to battle stations, checked the plot of the target's course, and took *U-333* to the surface. With a quarter moon to the east, he decided not to be the one silhouetted, so he positioned his boat, in a switch of strategy, between the coast and the target. From the bridge in the glow of the moonlight, he spotted a blacked-out ship running north. This would be a picnic — another target proceeding on a straight course.

With his makeshift sighting device Cremer aimed the boat at what appeared to be a small freighter. He could see the two masts, the midship superstructure, and the gun on the stern clearly outlined against the moon-lit sea.

He spoke into the bridge tube, "Course 349, speed nine knots. Open bow tubes. Range 600 yards. Launch one. Launch two."

Cremer watched the track of the first torpedo. At 30 seconds, a flash lit the sky, and the sound of the explosion boomed across the water. Flames shot up the forward mast. The ship wallowed, and within minutes the last flame winked out as she disappeared into the sea. Cremer knew that there had been no time for a distress signal. He doubted if anyone had survived. Ship crews were killed by his attacks, that was war, but he always felt better if he could see people abandoning ship.

As *U-333* made its second attack of the night, another sub, *U-109*, slipped down the coast off Vero Beach. Captain Heinrich Bleichrodt had assured himself of a successful voyage, having sunk three ships in five days off Cape Canaveral. It was time to return across the Atlantic. The U-boat had just enough fuel, but he wanted to use up his three remaining torpedoes. Targets around Cape Canaveral had dried up the last couple of nights, so he decided to take *U-109* farther south. He proceeded on the surface a few miles beyond Bethel Shoal. From his vantage point on the bridge, he marveled at the lit-up coastline. The quarter moon shone to his back. Suddenly, he saw a shadow off the starboard bow — a big tanker. His lookouts had now seen her. One reported, "Captain, she appears to be lying still in the water. No movement. Nothing coming from her stack."

Bleichrodt could see she had a slight list. She must have been hit by another U-boat. He could not communicate with the other boats, only with Admiral Doenitz's headquarters in France, but he guessed there must be at

least two other U-boats along the Florida coast. He checked his watch —
4:00 a.m. With no other targets around, and dawn coming shortly, he prepared his boat to fire one torpedo — an easy shot on a still target.

The Captain launched the torpedo. He waited. No explosion, nothing.

"A God-damn dud!" he groaned, throwing up his hands. It wasn't the
first torpedo failure on this trip. "They send us 4,000 miles across the
ocean and give us shit."

Just then a plane appeared from the east, its blinking wing lights showing its path. Bleichrodt's first instinct was that his boat was about to be
attacked. But then he remembered that his charts showed an airport at Vero
Beach and that the plane must be making an approach.

"Prepare to submerge," the Captain ordered.

"Big tanker — inside course north — speed 12 knots — distance half
mile." Peter Cremer spoke through his bridge tube to the control room.
Just over an hour had passed since he had watched the small freighter go
down. He had kept *U-333* surfaced and in the same general area since the
moon, now behind clouds in the western sky, no longer illuminated the
water. Cremer fired two torpedoes, one after the other. From the bridge he
sensed that both hit midships, almost simultaneously. The tanker didn't
explode, but began to settle slowly.

"We got her; she's going down," he announced to his crew. "Good
night's work," then gave the command to submerge.

Cremer laid the boat on the bottom in 30 feet of water near St. Lucie
Shoal. He hoped he hadn't stirred up too much trouble. He wanted to lay
undetected during the coming daylight, rest up, and be ready for the next
night. Sinking this tanker replaced his remorse about wasting two torpedoes on the freighter when he realized how small she was. Forget it, he
told himself. This last target was legitimate and then some. With three
ships to his credit in one night, particularly in the shape his boat was in,
he would be back in Doenitz's good graces. The Paris dinner bill charged
to the Admiral would be forgotten. Cremer smiled at the thought.

When the *Kitsis*, wallowing in the tide under its load, bumped the Coast

Guard Station dock, Ottie looked up from the bilge and saw several Coast Guardsmen peering down at the mass of humanity jammed in the boat. Ottie climbed from the bilge and looked at his wristwatch — 5:30 a.m. The Coast Guardsmen secured the lines and then helped the *Java Arrow* crewmen, one by one, off the cruiser and walked them across the grass into the station. When the boat was empty, Ottie looked at Kit and commented, "We wanted some action. We got it."

"Yeah, I wasn't sure we'd make it."

"You did a hell of a job bringing her in," Ottie complimented Kit.

"The boat's a friggin' mess. Let's have a drink and go home." And with that Kit went below and reappeared with a half bottle of bourbon. He waved it at Ottie, "I think we deserve this," and swigged a mouthful.

He handed the bottle to Ottie who took a sip, felt the hot bitterness pour down his throat, and passed it on to Ward and Harvey. Another pass emptied the bottle, and Kit flipped it overboard. They watched it for a minute as it floated with the falling tide, bobbing out the inlet to the open sea.

"That's for the God-damn Germans!" declared Kit.

Peter Cremer and his crew's daytime rest ended quickly. His sound man reported a destroyer-type vessel approaching at high speed. Cremer knew the destroyer had pinpointed *U-333*'s location with her echo range device. He called his crew to battle stations, started the electric motors and began to move off to deeper water.

His log would record a frightening day:

> Destroyer moved toward us at high speed . . . ocean like a mirror. Waboos (depth charges) dropped . . . lost both depth rudders . . . changed to hand operation. The bilges filled. Boat sank like a rock . . . heard the waboos fall and they all came down near us . . . heard noises as if tanks were shot out . . . lost a great deal of our lighting and stuff came off the ceiling. . . . All controls and indicators are lost. The diesel air mast is leaking . . . we lost ship communication system. Intention: try with all means to get boat off the ground during the next attack. . . . Now electric motors have stopped.

At noon, after four hours of sleep, Ottie drove across the bridge to the beach. He parked his truck, picked up a pair of binoculars lying on the seat and walked up to the dune line. He raised the binoculars to his eyes and scanned the horizon to the southeast. There he saw a shape, the hazy silhouette of a ship. He watched. She wasn't moving; no smoke rose from her stack. Must be the *Java Arrow*, he thought. The crew was right; she hadn't sunk. Beyond the tanker, Ottie saw the top of a dark cloud. It looked like a summer thunderstorm, but not this time of year. It had to be smoke from a burning tanker, another victim from last night.

"OK you guys, roll out. We gotta a job to do."

Willard Hesse heard Sweeney's voice as if from a far distance. He opened his eyes and saw Sweeney standing over the cots. It was hot. It must be late afternoon. Where the hell was he? Then it came to him — the trip in on the fishing boat, squashed by his mates' bodies, sitting on the cockpit deck, rolling against each other as the boat swayed, people vomiting. Then water had begun to slosh into the cockpit. That had scared him. At the Coast Guard Station he had been checked by a doctor, fed, and with several of the guys led into what looked like a hangar, but it turned out to be a buoy repair shop. A bunch of cots had been set up in the middle. He had picked one, pulled off his shoes, peeled off his wet shirt and dungarees, and had fallen asleep.

Bill Swazy in the next cot asked, "What's up, Sweeney?"

"The Coast Guard's going crazy. We weren't the only ones hit last night. A freighter went down off of here, and a tanker is burning to the south. You can see the smoke from the beach. There must have been a couple of subs out there. We were lucky."

"We're not going back out to the ship, are we?" asked one of the guys.

"Yeah, that's what we're doing. She's still afloat. When the Coast Guard finally got out there to pick up the other lifeboat, they put Hennichen and some of the boys back on board to drop the anchor. That must have been about four a.m. They said she was a menace to navigation, just drifting up the coast. Then, the Coast Guard brought 'em all in."

"Where is everybody?" asked another voice.

"The guys with injuries were taken in a school bus to a hospital in West Palm Beach. The rest left a little while ago for Fort Lauderdale on a Navy bus. They'll probably be put on a train back to New York."

"What about Shera?" asked Willard.

"His body was found in the engine room. Fentress was in the companionway. The Coast Guard brought the bodies in."

"And they want us to go back out there?" asked the guy on the cot next to Willard.

"That's it." Sweeney stood, looking down on the men beginning to roll out of the cots. "The Coast Guard has rounded up a couple of tugs and is going to tow her to Fort Lauderdale. We'll stay with the ship while she gets towed."

"Yea, and get torpedoed again," griped another voice.

"The Coast Guard says they'll give us an escort," said Sweeney.

"Bullshit," someone mumbled.

Willard agreed. He'd had enough.

That night, almost 24 hours after they had been torpedoed, Captain Hennichen, Sweeney, and 12 crewmen, including Willard, stood with a Coast Guard Lieutenant and an old man in a T-shirt and dungarees on the dark bow of the *Java Arrow*. The old man held a welding torch in his hand. He had been rolled out of bed in Fort Pierce by the Coast Guard and with his welding gear brought out to the ship. His job was to cut the anchor chain at the six-fathom hackle where it would be tied off to the tow line. With the engine dead and no steam to drive the windlass, there was no way to lift the 4,000-pound anchor.

The ocean lay calm. Willard could hear the lap of the water against the hull and the hiss of the welding torch spewing gas, waiting to be ignited. The quarter moon hadn't appeared yet. The only light came from the stars and flashlights held by the Lieutenant and Sweeney. The two tugs, their silhouettes just barely visible, lay a hundred yards off the *Java Arrow* waiting to attach their lines for the tow.

The welder struck an arc and the acetylene torch flared into action. He applied the arc to a gigantic link of rusty chain. Red sparks flew. The intense blue flame from the torch lit up the bow, silhouetting the men. An eerie glow spread over the water.

Captain Hennichen asked the welder, "How long is this going to take?"

"Forty-five minutes or so to cut through this much iron," he answered.

Willard had felt all right on the ship in the dark, but now they might as well have shot off a flare signaling every U-boat at sea that "here we are," a lovely target, dead in the water. He wasn't the only nervous one. There was some whispering and grumbling among the men who stood off to the side, watching the welder slowly cutting through the chain link.

After a few minutes one of the men approached Sweeney, "We want off this son-of-a-bitch while that guy is welding. We sure as hell don't want to end up like Shera and Fentress."

Sweeney tried to convince the group to hang on for another hour, that the welding would be over by then, but the crew was adamant. Willard had mixed feelings. He was scared too, but didn't want to run away. The Captain finally agreed that any of the crew who wanted to could get off the ship. Several went over the side by the gangway and boarded the Coast Guard patrol boat. The boat then moved off.

Willard decided to stay and help the welder when he could, knowing the old guy was scared to death himself. Willard could see the welder's hands shake when he moved the torch. Finally, the welder cut through the link, extinguished his torch, and the safety of darkness returned.

The Coast Guard Lieutenant signaled the tugs with his flashlight to come alongside. The group who had fled to the patrol boat came back aboard. Willard and the rest of the crew began to prepare the lines for the tow.

That night *U-333* presented no threat to shipping despite the fears of the men aboard the damaged *Java Arrow*. Peter Cremer's only thought was survival. He moved throughout the boat, encouraging his men as they worked through the midnight hours.

Finally, the engine crew got the electric motors running. The electric hum, after hours of deadly silence, gave his men hope. Cremer was thankful again for the abilities and creativeness aboard his boat, already proven in the mid-Atlantic when the diesel had quit and after the ramming off Bermuda. The boat could now move to deeper water, eking out what juice was left in the batteries, while the rest of the repairs continued. He believed their attacker had moved off, but without the periscope he couldn't see unless he surfaced. He inched the boat quietly forward for an hour, gradually gaining more depth. Then he put her on the bottom and shut down the engines to conserve battery power. At some point, he must take the risk and surface for sufficient time to run the diesels and fully charge the batteries.

At mid-morning, with the boat still laying on the bottom, the sound man reported the props of an approaching vessel, probably a destroyer. Cremer considered the alternative of sitting still, hoping not to be found, or moving again. He knew the old World War I depth charges that the U.S. Navy was still using would not explode below 200 feet.

"Start electric motors," he ordered. The motors whined as they absorbed what little power was left in the batteries and began turning the propellers, inching the boat slowly eastward. *U-333* was now just off the bottom at the 150-feet depth. Then the "waboos" began to fall, exploding all around them. The explosions continued at intervals all morning rattling the boat and the crew. More leaks sprung, spraying the sweating crew with salt water, but the sub kept moving closer to the magic depth. Shortly after noon, the arrow on the depth recorder reached 200 foot.

Cremer ordered, "Stop all engines." The boat settled on the bottom. No more waboos fell.

Cremer checked with the sound man who sat in his cubicle with headphones covering his ears, twisting dials, listening.

"Sir," he said to Cremer, "I hear engines idling at three-hundred yards." The enemy was still there. Now it was a case of out-waiting him.

As evening approached, Cremer assessed his situation. Too much water had leaked into the boat. The oxygen bottles were nearly empty. The crew couldn't get sufficient air and were at the end of their physical strength. The men breathed in gasps and jerks and were bathed in sweat. He felt like they were shut in a steel cage with the roof threatening to cave in at any moment.

In darkness, Cremer made the only move he could. He poked the conning tower above the surface to take in fresh air and charge the batteries. He had no idea where his attacker lay, but he was desperate. From the bridge he scanned the horizon. The dark silhouette of a destroyer lay still in the water a little over a mile away. It was too close for him to crank up the diesels and charge the batteries. He replenished the boat's air and, using what little juice was left, submerged.

The next day, Cremer kept his boat on the bottom while the crew

Lieutenant Commander Peter Cremer, upon the triumphant return of *U-333* to U-boat pens at La Rochelle, France, May 26, 1942, after sinking four ships. Cremer was later presented the Knight's Cross, one of Germany's highest military honors.   *Peter Cremer*

completed the repairs. That night he surfaced and discovered with relief that his pursuer had left. The other good news was that a saddle fuel tank he thought torn had only minor leaks. Cremer charged the batteries, made a test dive, and found his boat reasonably tight. Using the diesels, he moved her on the surface, 60 miles out to sea. The sub was now beyond the reach of the enemy and ready to travel on the surface day and night. With economic use of the remaining diesel fuel, *U-333* would be able to cover 250 miles a day.

On May 10, well beyond the Bahamas and out into the Atlantic, a look-out spotted, through drizzling rain, a lone freighter moving perpendicular to their course. Cremer climbed to the bridge from the control room. The rain poured off his slicker. What a choice target, he thought — she can't see us in this weather.

After the attack, back in the dryness of his cramped quarters, he wrote in his log:

> Freighter inside. . . . Perfect for me after waboo attack of a few days ago. Answer to a prayer. Had him at great delight for breakfast. . . . Hit mid-ships . . . bridge and superstructure flew through the air. Crew abandoned ship. Turned over with keel up. This is salve for our waboo wounds.

While Peter Cremer reveled in his final conquest, Willard Hesse stood on the stern watching as two tugs maneuvered the *Java Arrow* through the inlet at Fort Lauderdale into Port Everglades. Looking beyond the jetties, Willard saw the distant figures of girls sunning themselves on the beaches.

The trip to Fort Lauderdale had taken four tedious days covering a hundred sea miles. With the gash in its side, the ship yawed badly; the tugs frequently repositioned themselves as they crept along. A Coast Guard patrol boat provided escort. Over all, it had been a quiet journey except for the first day. Then they had passed within a couple of miles of a destroyer lobbing depth charges, presumably at a sub.

Willard thought of going home. He would have lots to tell, if he was allowed to say anything. Sweeney had heard that they were to be put on a train north within a couple of days. Willard could hardly wait.

The rumor was that the *Java Arrow* would have her hull repaired at Port Everglades, and then her steam engine replaced with a diesel at some shipyard up east. Willard figured he might be back on her in a year. He thought they had been lucky that she hadn't sunk, lucky they weren't carrying liquid fuel in their cargo tanks, lucky, he supposed, they had lost only two men. After his visit home, he would have to face going back on another ship, knowing that the subs would still be out there.

On May 26, almost two months to the day from his departure, Peter Cremer and *U-333* entered the port at La Rochelle. As the boat cut through the oily waters, the crew could see the hills, ablaze with spring flowers, beyond the mammoth U-boat pens.

Peter Cremer, with a full beard and wearing his white Commander's hat, stood erect on the bridge of the conning tower with his officers. A tingle rippled through his body as the submarine, with her crunched bow, smashed conning tower, and bent periscope glided triumphantly into the harbor. Above his head, four pennants fluttered from the mast, one for each of the ships torpedoed. We did it, despite what happened, he thought.

Below, his crew stood at attention on the deck. He was proud of these men. He had led them, and they had performed. But his foremost thought, shared with the rest of the crew, was, "Let's get this pomp and ceremony over so we can put our feet on dry land."

On the bunker dock, high-ranking German officers in elegant uniforms, with swastikas on their caps, watched approvingly. Band music boomed across the water. Photographers snapped their cameras. Pretty girls, some in nurses uniforms, some in flowing dresses, raised their arms and tossed flowers toward the boat.

A hero had returned from the far shore. Two weeks later Admiral Doenitz presented Lieutenant Commander Peter Cremer the Knight's Cross, one of Germany's highest military honors.

Chapter 17

Heavenly Twins
1989

RIVING HOME FROM the German Naval Memorial that Sunday afternoon after dropping off the two fellows who had gone with us, Peter asked, "Your father has Alzheimer's, you said. How is he?"

"No change. He hasn't recognized my mother or me for several years."

"Alzheimer's is a terrible disease."

We drove on in silence.

That night in my room I was tired, but couldn't sleep. The day had been interesting, but in the end, depressing — both the Naval Memorial and coming to the realization that Peter was not quite as robust as he liked to portray. Triggered by Peter's question about Dad, I thought about my father lying mindless in the Pavilion at Shell Point, and that a time had existed when I had never even heard the word Alzheimer's. Uncle Howard, not Dad, provided the first introduction to the disease. Both were now fighting a different kind of battle from those they had fought during the war.

In the fall of 1972, Katharine and I stood in the upstairs guest room of Aunt Pye and Uncle Howard's house on their 400-acre farm near Lewisburg, West Virginia. We were on a rare vacation without the children and had driven a car up from Florida for Mom and Dad, who had a cabin in the woods nearby. Dressing for dinner, I looked out the window at the reds and yellows of fall dotting the ridge beyond the pasture.

"Do you notice anything different about Uncle Howard?" Katharine asked, as she stood in front of the mirror, combing her short brown hair.

I hesitated, "He seems quieter." What I meant was that his aggressiveness had disappeared. He hadn't razzed me since we had been at the farm.

"Maybe he's mellowed with age," I said. He and Dad were now 65, but that didn't seem so old.

"Maybe," Katharine replied, "But it's interesting we've both noticed the same thing. He's not the Uncle Howard I've known."

I would not have said anything, just let the worry turn over in my mind and then tuck it away. But Katharine had expressed what we both felt.

A year later we had an explanation. We sat at dinner with Aunt Pye and Uncle Howard at the Boar's Head Inn in Charlottesville, Virginia. Uncle Howard was undergoing medical tests at the University of Virginia Hospital. By chance, we were in Charlottesville at the same time. I had talked my company into sending me to my alma mater for a three-day computer course, and Katharine had come along for the fun. Aunt Pye, in her frank, funny manner, explained the situation, right there at the table.

"George has become rattle-brained, that's all. I guess we all get that way sooner or later."

Aunt Pye's nickname for Uncle Howard was "George" from the expression, "Let George do it." She also liked to compare him to Philip, Queen Elizabeth's husband. There was a remarkable resemblance; both were handsome men.

I never knew what Aunt Pye was going to say, and I felt embarrassed by her remarks at the table. I glanced at Uncle Howard, who was completing his second bourbon and water. This once-confident man looked at me from across the table. The playful hint of a smile returned for a moment.

"Don't pay attention to Pye," he said. "The doctors don't know a damn thing." He took a sip from his highball glass then switched subjects. "Your father still shooting holes-in-one? He's getting pretty damn good on the golf course. I'm going there this winter and whip him."

"He plays every day. Knocks the heck out of the ball, but still has problems with his putting. With the Florida Sporting Goods gone, golf has pretty much been his life," I replied.

"Well, he gets more practice than I do, that's for sure." Uncle Howard took another sip.

Later, back in our hotel room, Katharine told me about the conversation she had with Aunt Pye in the ladies' room after dinner.

Aunt Pye had explained, "Howard no longer remembers names. He forgets everything he is supposed to do. He sometimes makes lists to remind himself. And yet he's healthy as a bull. When the doctors asked him questions, he got huffy, told them he could read fine, said his judgment was still pretty damn good, he was just forgetful. The doctors asked if he ever got lost, if he could dress himself. He has none of those kinds of problems, but he can hardly remember his own name."

Katharine asked what kind of tests they had run on him. Aunt Pye answered, "The whole kit and caboodle: brain scan, skull films, chemical profiles, and a psychiatric exam. They didn't show anything, Dear. The conclusion was dementia of an unknown cause, whatever the heck that means."

After the trip to Charlottesville, Aunt Pye and Uncle Howard sold the farm, rented a small house in Lewisburg, and started coming to Vero Beach for the winters. Aunt Pye wanted the "heavenly twins," as she called Uncle Howard and Dad, to have some time together. They had always had a close relationship. Their raucous birthday parties were legendary in the family, and Dad always had been there when tough decisions were to be made regarding the family business.

Their differences in personality, and Uncle Howard's successes and lifestyle, never seemed to get in the way. When they were growing up, they had competed on the athletic fields and sailed against each other during the summers. I knew from their stories, their kidding, and their trophies that they were both excellent athletes. They must have established an early equality that the later differences in their lives couldn't change. At home, we had a picture of them when they were three, together in little boy sailor suits. There was no question who was who. Uncle Howard appeared immaculate, everything in place; Dad looked rumpled, shirttail out, like he had been in a wrestling match.

In Vero the next winter the heavenly twins played golf and fished. But things had changed. Uncle Howard could no longer add, and Dad would keep his golf score. One Sunday at the Sebastian Inlet, casting for bluefish from a boat, I watched Dad telling Uncle Howard how to handle the spinning rod.

"Howard, you have to pull the bail down. Howard, turn the rod over. The reel is on the bottom." Sometimes Dad would just reach over and turn the rod himself. Uncle Howard didn't say a thing.

During the cocktail conversation at the Riomar Club, according to my mother, Uncle Howard still held his own. Aunt Pye's comment was, "In that crowd you could speak Chinese and no one would know the difference."

Then one night we received a call from Mom. That morning Uncle Howard had wandered out of the house that they were renting, and Aunt Pye couldn't find him. She frantically called Dad. He got in the jeep and started driving around the island. A half hour later he found his brother, dressed as if he were going to play golf, walking down the side of A1A with cars whizzing past. Within two days, Aunt Pye packed up the Mercedes and drove Uncle Howard back to West Virginia. I never saw him again.

My dad also had a problem, but of a different sort. He was drinking too much. This had been going on since he and Mom had left Kanawha Acres, sold the Florida Sporting Goods, and moved into my grandmother's house in Riomar near the beach. While golf gave Dad an interest, it compounded the problem. The golf-resort atmosphere tended to be conducive to drinking; lunch at the club, cocktail parties, and people with time on their hands. Dad associated with men who had been business successes, presidents of corporations, and who talked about it in their retirement. I began to sense a sadness in Dad. Was he assessing his life and coming up short? Was he comparing himself to these men, or, in reality, did golf bore him? Worried about him, my Mom reacted by matching him drink for drink, but with "one ouncers."

Katharine and I became concerned about both of them. Dad held his liquor well, but family dinners became difficult. We would rush to get the food on the table so there wasn't time for another drink. Dad never became boisterous, but he slurred his words. His stability, the thing we loved the most and depended on, seemed to disappear.

I was so tuned to his personality, any change, even minor, disturbed me. I tried to ignore the situation, but Mom made it difficult. She kept yipping at him, "Kit, you've had enough."

When Dad ignored her she would go get another "one-ouncer." She never hesitated to speak her mind, and the alcohol accentuated this tendency. Had Dad and Mom become alcoholics? I didn't know and didn't want to find out.

Then, an incident occurred that I would not hear about for several years until Buck, our oldest son, felt sufficiently comfortable to tell me. I think he was afraid to worry me at the time. He had been 17 and had gone on a boat trip with Mom and Dad, "Nana and Gramps" as he called them. They were in Gramps's 22-foot Aquasport, which had followed a series of boats over the years and had to be about *Kitsis VIII* or *IX*. They were off Cape Florida, heading from Everglades City to Islamorada Key, cutting across Florida Bay. The location couldn't have been far from where Dad and I had tangled with that tarpon when I, too, was 17.

Their trip started in Vero Beach; they had gone through the cross-state canal, across Lake Okeechobee to Fort Myers and down around the tip of Florida to the Keys. The boat had no sleeping quarters, so they had docked at night near motels. The boat ran at 25 knots, allowing them to make long runs. However, Dad had not made this particular trip in 20 years.

Buck stood at the console with Dad; my mom sat in the stern reading a paperback mystery. They were running a compass course, trying to hit a buoy that would put them in sight of the radio tower at Islamorada. A chart lay on the console by the windscreen. Dad, with one hand on the wheel, kept picking up the chart and looking at it. As Buck watched the compass, he saw they were heading several degrees to the east of the course they had plotted in pencil on the chart.

"Gramps, are we off course?" asked Buck.

"No," said Dad. He picked up the chart again.

A couple of minutes went by. Buck looked at the compass. He hesitated, then asked, "Gramps, did you decide to swing a little bit east?"

"No."

"Well, that's where we're heading."

"No, we're not," and Dad glanced at the compass and looked at the chart.

Buck didn't say anything. He stared at his grandfather's face and saw something he had never seen before — confusion, almost fear.

My dad put the chart down and said, "Buck, you take the wheel. You know how to run a course. I've taught you well."

Buck told me that Dad went back to the stern and sat in a deck chair next to Mom. She put down her book and patted his leg. She knew that this day would come.

Shortly after the cruise, my mother began to talk about she and Dad entering a retirement center, one with extended medical care. I thought she was crazy and all but told her so. Dad was now 70; she was 63. They seemed in good health. Buck may have noticed changes in Dad, but I hadn't. There was no such place near Vero. Feeling that they were giving up, accepting old age, I would argue with her, "Mom, you all are too young to go into a retirement place, a nursing home, to move away. You don't want to leave your friends in Vero Beach. What about us? You won't get to see the kids like you do now."

She would answer, "Rody, we're getting older whether you accept that or not. We want to take care of ourselves. We don't want to ever put you and Katharine in a position where you feel you must have either your dad or me come live with you."

I said all this was silly. But of course, Mom had watched what had happened to Uncle Howard who, by then, Aunt Pye had committed to a West Virginia state mental hospital.

Mom always had a fear of medical matters which I presumed went back to Dad's ulcer condition. It would be Aunt Pye who, some years later, would finally tell me why. I had dropped by Lewisburg to see her on my way back to Florida from a business trip. Aunt Pye and I were sitting on the back yard of the General Lewis Inn having a drink. I realized that I had the opportunity to find out something that I had ignored all my life. I guess I had reached an age where I felt a responsibility for knowing what had gone on in the family. I got up my nerve, put my beer down, and asked, "Aunt Pye, did my dad's stomach operation and the death of my grandmother, Dad's mother, somehow take place about the same time?"

"I've wondered when you were going to ask," she replied. "Your mother would never talk. It's time you knew some things."

She took a sip of her bourbon and water and continued, "Your father was having stomach troubles and their doctor wanted to treat it a little longer, but Mrs. Johnson insisted that Kit go to Baltimore to see a surgeon recommended by some of her fancy Philadelphia friends. Kit and Sis weren't sure that was necessary. Your mother was twenty-three, and you didn't say no to Mrs. Johnson."

"I can remember her vaguely, Aunt Pye, from when I was three or four. She was "Gan Gan" to me. And you and Mom called her Mrs. Johnson?"

"Yes. She was a tough one, but then maybe she had reason to be. She had lost her husband, your grandfather, to ulcers when Howard and Kit were fourteen. Of course, your Uncle Charles and Uncle Rodolph were a little older. She raised the four boys and got them through college, except for Kit, who after his poor academic performance at Pomfret and Princeton Prep, she sent to technical school for a year. Then your Uncle Rodolph died in 1930, the year your mother and father were married. He had ulcers too, had an appendicitis attack, and the doctor didn't realize it."

I knew some of this, but had never explored it. "What really caused Dad's problems at the Charleston Electric?"

"With his father gone, a family friend had been running the business. It was during the Depression. The coal mines weren't doing well and nobody was buying washing machines or stoves. Mrs. Johnson decided the family friend had to be replaced. With the rest of the boys in college or out gallivanting around the world, it was up to Kit to fire the family friend. It was more than he could handle."

"What happened in Baltimore?" I took a swallow of my beer.

Aunt Pye sipped her drink. "That twit of a doctor insisted that most of Kit's stomach be removed. The idea was that the stomach secretes acids that cause ulcers — no stomach, no acid, no ulcers. And he went on to say, not to Sis, but to Mrs. Johnson, that if something wasn't done, your father would die. So they went ahead with the surgery, and Kit came out of the operating room in pretty good shape, but your mother was a nervous wreck. Mrs. Johnson was having some stomach problems of her own. This doctor thought she had some kind of blockage of the intestine. He decided that exploratory surgery was necessary. That was a couple of days after Kit's operation. He didn't find anything, and she came out of the operation very weak. He said she was fine and went off on a holiday. Three days later she died. Sis had to tell Kit that his mother was dead."

"Judas Priest, I didn't realize all that!"

"After Kit recovered from the surgery, you all moved to Florida."

I took a swig of my beer. For the first time, I had an appreciation for what my parents had been through and now could better understand some of Mom's fears of medical situations.

Mom had heard about Shell Point Village, located across the state in Fort Myers. We made a Sunday excursion. The place looked impressive, similar to the most elegant of condominium complexes. There were a variety of buildings and immaculate lawns, situated in a beautiful location on the Caloosahatchee River. We toured the medical facility and nursing home, where you went if you were too ill or too old to take care of yourself. A lot of old people were sitting around in bathrobes.

Apparently, you bought an apartment, paid a monthly fee, and were guaranteed care for the rest of your life. However, when you died, the place kept your money. It didn't sound like a great deal to me, and the people I saw walking around the place, even outside the nursing facility, seemed much older than Mom and Dad.

On our tour we saw a tarpon roll in the waterway. Mom immediately told Dad, "You could have your boat here. Looks like the fishing would be good." He barely nodded.

I said to Mom, "If you all are going to do this, it's probably the right place. But you don't need to rush into it."

"Rody, these places don't take you after you become ill. You have to be in good health going in."

Three months later, in the summer of 1977, Mom and Dad moved to Shell Point to a third-story, two-bedroom apartment with a porch overlooking the mangroves and the Caloosahatchee River. They took with them a limited amount of furniture and the boat. Their bank and their lawyer objected to the move, doubting the financial stability of the facility. The place was owned by the Christian Missionary Alliance, a Presbyterian spin-off and was financed by short-term notes from its church members.

And we moved as well, temporarily to Palo Alto, California. I had been assigned to a project which meant commuting to California every other week to monitor the progress of three electronics manufacturers. Our company had been chosen by the Iranian government to coordinate the development of a gigantic electronic eavesdropping system to monitor the military activities of its neighbors.

I got the idea that the whole family should move to Palo Alto; it would be a great adventure. After a couple of months of persuasion, Katharine and the children had reluctantly agreed. We set off in a Mercury Monarch, pulling a U-Haul rental trailer. I was at the wheel, with Charlie, age six, between Katharine and me in the front seat. In the back sat Buck, 18, Mark, 16, and Kit, their sister, 14. God was with us, and Allah as well, considering the project, because we made the seven-day cross-country trip without killing each other.

We found a house to rent on a tree-lined street across from an elementary school for Charlie and within a bicycle ride of Palo Alto High School. The children, much to our surprise, thrived in this Stanford-oriented environment where the quality of education was foremost; Katharine had exposure to more sophisticated art training; and I congratulated myself on having done this wonderful thing for my family. But, maybe, what I had really done was to find an escape from the worries about my parents.

While we were in Palo Alto, Mom and Dad came to visit. Dad had always talked about going to Alaska, so he and I flew up for a week, leaving Mom in Palo Alto with Katharine and the children. I hadn't seen my Dad in a year except for a couple of quick business trips back to Florida.

Dad and I stayed in a cabin on the shore of Lake Clark, a hundred miles west of Anchorage. Each morning we flew in a Cessna float plane with our pilot guide and two other fishermen to a different location in southeast Alaska. We found red salmon that, by the millions, migrated inland in early August from the Bering Sea to Lake Iliamna and its neighboring rivers and streams.

One evening I was in the cabin, lying on my cot. A Coleman lantern lit the room. A fire burned in the wood stove. In a corner our waders, with a puddle of water around them, dried next to Dad's fly rod and my spinning rod. Dad had gone to the outhouse a couple of cabins away. After a few minutes I was wondering about him, when the door banged and he came in. He wore a blue stocking cap with gray hair sprouting out the edges, his old Coast Guard pea jacket, dungarees, and sneakers. He had a cigarette hanging out of his mouth and his glasses sitting on his nose.

"I can't find the crapper. Did they move it?"

"Don't think so, Pappy. Let's go see." I put on my jacket, slipped into my boots, and led the way to the outhouse. Despite being 9 p.m., it was almost as light as day.

"Here, it is."

"Yeah. Why couldn't I find it?" He went in and slammed the door. I waited. What was going on? I knew he was having a little trouble. When we were fishing, he got tired after a few casts, and he'd go sit on a rock holding his fly rod across his knees, watching me and the other guys fish.

"You OK?" I'd ask, and he would answer, "Fine."

I was also afraid Dad was going to burn the cabin down, as he kept leaving his cigarettes on the edge of boxes. I would show him the cigarette, and he would go pick it up.

He came out of the john and we walked to the cabin. We could see the black waters of the lake and the silhouettes of the mountains rising on the other side. The two float planes sat in the water in front of us, the back of their pontoons resting on the sandy edge of the lakeshore.

We entered the cabin. He sat down, pulled his clothes off, hung them over a chair, and lay down on his cot in his shorts and T-shirt. He put his cigarette on the ash tray, and closed his eyes. I got up and went over and snuffed out the cigarette, took his glasses off of him and laid them on the box. He didn't move.

"Night Pappy," I murmured, and curled up on my bunk to read. But I couldn't read. I was thinking of Dad and what he had done earlier, after supper. A group of fishermen had been sitting out in front of the main lodge, smoking and telling stories. They had been talking about bear hunting. Dad joined them. He spoke and the men, all younger, turned and listened. I stood on the periphery of the group. Dad didn't generally tell stories; he mostly listened. But here he was.

"We were off Grand Bahama in '36. Damnedest storm I ever saw. Winds fifty knots from the southwest. No lee for the boat. We were pounded all night. Couldn't sleep. Just had to keep changing the lines." And so on.

Dad had just popped in with his story. The men began to clear their throats and look at each other. I became flushed in the face as he went on and on. I'd never seen him do anything like this, not even at Camp Imperial. I knew he had drunk only a couple of beers before dinner so it wasn't alcohol. Finally, I excused myself, stepped into the circle of men, grasped him by the arm, and said, "Pappy, time to hit the sack."

He stopped, looked at me, and replied, "OK."

He got up and, with me gently holding his arm, told his audience "good night." We headed for the cabin. As we walked, I said to him, "I've never heard that story before."

"What story?" he'd asked.

I lay on the cot, troubled. I had been embarrassed in front of those men by my father. What was wrong with me? But the real problem was that I could no longer ignore my dad's situation. I couldn't rationalize anymore that he just was getting a little senile and his drinking probably had made it worse. I had to accept that Dad's behavior tracked Uncle Howard's.

Back in Vero Beach, after our one-year stay in Palo Alto, Katharine and I were reading out on the porch. Katharine came across an article in *Ladies Home Journal*, by Rita Hayworth's daughter describing a disease her mother had, called Alzheimer's, and its symptoms were all too familiar. Katharine and I stayed up late that night talking. Shortly afterwards we went to see the family doctor to talk about Dad. Yes, the doctor had heard about Alzheimer's, but knew very little about it.

In the meantime, the reports from Mom at Shell Point indicated that Dad was becoming more forgetful. We decided to take Mom and Dad and our three boys to Islamorada in the Keys to relive the fun times we had enjoyed there in the past. One afternoon the two older boys were bone-fishing with a guide. Katharine said she would stay with Dad at the motel so Mom could have a break and go fishing with Charlie and me. While we were gone, Dad became agitated. He paced the motel room, constantly asking where Sissy was.

Katharine tried to cajole him, "Don't you want to lie down, Dad, and watch TV?"

"No, I want Sissy. Where is Sissy?"
"She's fishing with Rody and Charlie."
"I want Sissy."
By the time we returned three hours later Katharine was almost out of her mind. She told me later, "I now know what your mother is going through. It's worse than taking care of a two-year-old."

With Mom and Dad across the state, we had been removed from what was going on with my father. I responded to the immediacy of telephone calls, but Mom was not crying for help. Like Aunt Pye had with Uncle Howard, she was handling the situation. When I hung up after talking with Mom, I plunged back into the demands of my own life. Our daughter, Kit, married at 18, gave us some worries; the two older boys were in college, and with Charlie we were involved in Little League three nights a week. Add a *New York Times* newsroom computer project with technical problems that I was managing, and I had lots of escapes from the situation at Shell Point.

Looking back, I've wondered what I could have done. Should I have talked with Dad about how he felt as his mind went? At times, learning that Alzheimer's is hereditary, whenever I forgot a name, I felt I might be getting the disease. Strangely enough, this kind of thinking occurred more frequently back when we were dealing with it.

In January 1979, Uncle Howard died in Denmar State Hospital in Marlington, West Virginia. He had deteriorated to the point that he refused to eat and was fed by tubes. The hospital discussed his situation with Aunt Pye and, based on a living will that had been made several years earlier, the doctors removed the tubes. The final diagnosis on Uncle Howard's medical report: Alzheimer's disease.

Shortly afterwards, Katharine and I brought Mom over to Vero. We wanted to get her away for a few days. Dad had been left in the care of a nurse. When we arrived home late in the evening, a message was waiting for Mom to call Shell Point. I dialed the number and handed her the phone.

"Sue, is everything all right?" Mom put her cigarette out in the ashtray by the phone. I knew she was talking to Dad's nurse. There was silence.

"Did he hurt you?" Mom asked. More silence.

"That's all you could do, Sue. Thank you." Mom hung up.

My father had been moved to the Pavilion, in essence a nursing home, for the rest of his life. I had lost him. He may not have died like Uncle Howard, but as far as I was concerned he was gone.

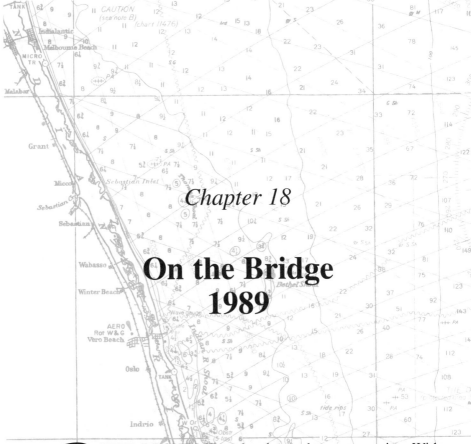

Chapter 18

On the Bridge
1989

ETER DROVE ME to the airport the next morning. With a full day of business ahead, he seemed rejuvenated despite our trip to the Naval Memorial, and I felt much the same way. My depressing thoughts of the previous night were put aside as if they had been a bad dream. I had a wonderful time with Peter, plus answers for all the questions I had listed on my yellow pad.

We roared through suburban Hamburg. Peter, with the dash of the daring U-boat Commander, raced the stoplights turning yellow, calling them "taxi green." He chuckled as he told me about a company-provided chauffeur he once had whose license had been suspended because of drunk driving. Peter chauffeured the chauffeur so he wouldn't be fired.

Peter pulled up at the entrance of the Hamburg airport. We retrieved my bags from his trunk, I thanked him for all that he had done for me, we shook hands, and he drove off.

My flight to Frankfurt and the change of planes went smoothly. Security for some reason seemed lighter. Headed back across the

Atlantic, settled next to a window, I dozed. I woke up, remembering something Peter had told me in his back yard.

"Family tradition gives backbone. It keeps you on the bridge by yourself when things are tough. You fight, you die, but you don't give up."

I thought about his obsession with family background and that only in wartime could a man prove such a philosophy as dramatically as Peter did. Sitting there I considered his war experiences, remembering what I had read in his book and the stories he had told me during the last four days.

Peter could have lost his life several times on the Florida trip. He had been bombed leaving France, rammed by a tanker off Bermuda, and attacked by a corvette, but the only time he had ever been wounded happened off the West African town of Freeport in October 1942.

He had told me this story. "We were laying on the surface at night observing the port. Suddenly, I saw a British destroyer escort approaching at great speed. She must have had radar. There is no other way she could have seen us. There was no time to dive or man the forward gun. She was on us, machine guns raking the boat, a searchlight flooding our conning tower, trying to ram us at full speed."

Peter turned *U-333* inside the attacker, the British corvette HMS *Crocus*, and the two boats had collided in a side-by-side struggle. Showers of metal splinters penetrated Peter's arms and chest, but he stayed on the bridge. He miraculously outmaneuvered his foe and submerged. His crew carried him to his bunk. During the battle, three of his men died and one disappeared overboard.

"The chief engineer removed a metal splinter from my chest with a set of pliers. I was losing blood and my left side was paralyzed. Three days later we rendezvoused with a Milch Cow. She had a doctor on board, thank God! The doctor, he saved my life," recounted Peter.

But there had been other close calls. A year after recovering from his wounds, Peter and *U-333* had joined a wolf pack to ambush an Allied convoy near the Azores. *U-333* positioned herself and prepared to launch a salvo of torpedoes. A frigate turned on her and, in a flurry of depth charges, ran over her while she maneuvered at periscope depth.

Peter described the action. "It was like being rammed by that tanker off Bermuda, but worse. The collision destroyed the periscope, knocked one of the diesels off its block, and damaged the controls. We could not balance the boat. She was slipping backwards into the depths."

But Peter had inspired his crew to perform another miracle, enabling the boat to be sufficiently repaired to crawl back to port.

In early 1944, while U.S. forces struggled in Italy and the Russians took advantage of winter to push back the Germans, *U-333* entered the North Channel between Ireland and England — the convoy path into Great Britain. She crept into the ten-mile-wide, heavily mined channel, and then was discovered by a patrol plane. A group of destroyer escorts pounced on her and threw an array of depth charges. Peter took his only recourse; he lay the sub silently on the shallow bottom. This worked. The attackers lost her and left.

"I gave the order to surface, but the boat would not budge. She lay stuck in the mud on the bottom." He smiled as he told me this. "I blew the tanks and applied full power to the electric motors. Nothing. Then I had a thought. I ran the crew, back and forth, leaping through bulkheads, from bow to stern and back again. The boat rocked slightly, the suction broke, and we rose to the surface. This was why the men liked to be on my boat. They said I was a cat of nine lives." He then returned to port — no ships sunk, but alive.

"I trained the hell out of the crew and they hated it. But they loved me when we were being attacked," Peter added.

After the Allied invasion of Normandy in June 1944, Peter left *U-333*. Doenitz had ordered him to the command of a Type XXI class submarine, newly developed to possess the speed, payload, and underwater capability that supposedly would reverse the fortunes of Germany's U-boat war. By this time, the Allies were out-producing Germany in war matériel, aircraft, ships, and submarines. The breaking of the German military codes early in the war, as well as the Allied use of radar, had decimated the German war machine.

Peter explained his feelings about the new assignment. "I was excited, but did not want to leave *U-333* with its three little fishies on the conning tower. On the train back to Germany, I heard that *U-333* had been sunk by a British destroyer off the west end of England. I felt very bad. Everyone was lost. If I had been with her, could I have made a difference? I don't know."

But Peter seemed to have put *U-333* behind him. In October 1944, he arrived in Hamburg and found *U-2519* still very much under construction and weeks away from sea trials. Her new equipment was advanced, more complicated than that of the *U-333*, and took longer than expected to check out and correct. *U-2519* was commissioned on November 15, 1944. Sea trials continued into April 1945.

Peter said that he was most frustrated with the delays, but the boat was wonderful. The sub could travel submerged at 17 knots compared to the *U-333*'s 7 knots. Her range extended 16,000 miles, sufficient to go to the tip of South America and back. She carried 24 torpedoes, 7 more than he had crammed into *U-333* for the Florida mission. *U-2519* could stay submerged for three days straight.

While *U-2519* was in dry dock for more work, the yard was bombed by the Allies on April 5. Knocked off her supports, the sub's periscope was damaged beyond repair, and her port ballast and fuel tanks were badly dented.

Peter described the sub's demise. "With the Allies closing in, my boat had still not seen the enemy. Then an Allied bomber dropped a bomb close by and the explosion toppled *U-2519* on her side. I would not go to sea again."

Peter's submarine days had come to an end, but he had continued to fight. In fact, he went to extremes to fight. Why? I could only rationalize that it was his loyalty to his comrades, certainly not to the Nazi regime.

Peter described his last war action. "I formed an anti-tank unit with some of my crew and joined the ground forces defending against the British. We used what you call a bazooka. We destroyed twenty-four tanks."

Germany surrendered on May 8, 1945. The war in Europe was over.

I shifted in my seat and looked down at the white puffy clouds and sea below. It came to me that the jet's course back to Miami probably followed *U-333*'s track to Florida all those years ago. I couldn't stop thinking about Peter and the war.

On April 30, 1945, Hitler appointed Admiral Doenitz as his successor and then committed suicide. Peter and his submariners were fighting in the vicinity of Doenitz's headquarters so they joined their Admiral as his security guard. Hitler's Gestapo and SS leader, Heinrich Himmler, thought he should have succeeded Hitler and arrived in the darkness at Doenitz's headquarters for a showdown.

Peter explained, "The Admiral told me, 'Keep him away from me.' I had a pistol in my pocket ready to use as I met this man and his SS troops. My men were in the woods behind me with orders to shoot if there was trouble. But there was none. Himmler backed down. He seemed like a nice man, a small-town teacher with glasses on his nose. You do not think he can do those things." He was referring, of course, to Himmler's role in the Jewish atrocities.

Within a week, Doenitz surrendered Germany to the Allied Forces.

However, Peter's adventures did not end. The Cold War gave him another opportunity to apply his "on the bridge" philosophy. In his back yard, he had shared yet another incident with me.

"There is a story that I was not allowed to put in my book. My editor thought it too sensitive since the Russian spy who was involved is still alive. Maybe you are interested?" Peter asked. I assured him I was and felt flattered that I was being taken into some kind of confidence.

"When the war ended, British Naval Intelligence assigned two interrogators to watch over me, to make sure I did not go over to the Russians. One of these men became my friend, the one that helped me find the job with British Petroleum."

Peter shifted in the lawn chair and revealed, "My other interrogator, a young British naval officer, was a Russian spy."

"A Russian spy?" I asked. "How did you know?"

"The British put him in jail long after I knew him. But the Russians helped him escape; he lives in Russia now. For five care packages of food, he asked me to go into East Germany to get information on a Russian shipyard. I was hungry. I would do anything for food. I rode underneath a coal train across the border with guards shining flashlights all around me. I bribed my way into the shipyard with cigarettes, but there was nothing to report, only minesweepers being repaired. I didn't know why I was sent for this unimportant information. On the way back I came on a railroad wagon and decided to climb in and rest. I woke to hear Russian soldiers approaching through the dark. I slipped away and escaped over a hill with a searchlight sweeping across it. I think this British naval officer had sent me across the border so I could be captured by the Russians. They wanted my submarine warfare knowledge."

I had trouble understanding this story at first. I later learned that Peter's spy was George Blake, who with Kim Philby and Dwight Burgess, were the famed double agents of British Intelligence who also spied for the Russian KGB. The British arrested Blake in Berlin in 1961 for espionage. He had given the Russians information on Western agents in Europe. He also had exposed the CIA's secret tunnel under the Berlin Wall which was used to tap East German telephone lines to gather Russian military information. After Blake told the Russians about the tunnel, they fed false information to the West. Blake received a 40-year sentence, but in 1966 made an unbelievable escape from a London prison. The KGB got credit for the escape, but a renegade Irishman, Sean Brooke, in a book written in 1970, claimed he masterminded the getaway. Blake now lives with his Russian wife and son in Moscow.

As I sat on the plane, I felt that Peter experienced more heroic times in his life than anybody I had ever known — that's, of course, what fascinated me. But as I thought about it, his words applied to more than just war; they fit the more normal aspects of one's life as well. An incident popped into my head which certainly wasn't heroic in the wartime sense, but was a time when Dad helped me to learn a life's lesson of how to "stay on the bridge."

When it was time to go to college, all I had ever heard about was Cornell, so I went. My uncles had taken engineering there and expected me to follow their path that would lead to the family business in West Virginia.

My Dad said in jest, "Don't worry about it. You might want to join me in the sporting goods business." What he had meant was that I should not consider joining the family business until I had proven myself elsewhere.

At Cornell I quickly developed a problem. My terrible grades — 30s in Physics — convinced me I was flunking out. I flew home for Thanksgiving, a trip that stretched the budget. I sat with my mom and dad on the front porch at Kanawha Acres and told them my sad tale of studying hard, but without results.

Dad listened for a few minutes. Then he spoke. This was unusual because I had always looked to my mom to solve growing-up problems.

"Rody," he said, "you want to fail."

I started to protest, but he quieted me with a slight raise of his hand.

"You're not studying; you're only going through the motions. It's gotten tough and you've given up. You think you have an excuse because you're putting in the hours on the books."

I listened, and suddenly I knew he had hit the truth. "Dad, maybe you're right."

Dad told me to go back up to that school and really work. "You're not a quitter. After Thanksgiving dinner, let's go out to camp and do some quail shooting. We'll see what college life has done to your shooting eye."

My attitude improved, and so did my grades.

Peter had been a war hero. And so had Uncle Howard, according to his citations. With a pride similar to Peter's, Uncle Howard too could have expressed Peter's philosophy.

What about my dad? He never would have put the same feelings into words, but he had lived it. I thought about his run-in with the three German submarines. Peter said it could have never happened. But I believed Dad and Ottie. Both men knew the sea. They were certainly not the type to exaggerate. If they said it happened — it happened.

Through data on when and where U-boats had sunk ships in American waters, I developed a scenario of how three subs could have been together near Bethel Shoal. According to the *Miami Herald* clipping that had been in my baby book and that Mom had sent me, Dad and Ottie saw the three subs on July 17, 1942. By then, Doenitz had shifted the U-boats to the Gulf of Mexico to attack the tanker traffic off Texas and New Orleans. But to get into the Gulf the subs still had to pass along the Florida East Coast. *U-67* torpedoed four ships in the Gulf between July 6 and July 13. *U-171* torpedoed two ships after July 26, and *U-166* torpedoed one on July 30. *U-166* and *U-171* may have been heading for the Gulf, and *U-67* may have been heading back to France. These three boats could have rendezvoused at Bethel Shoal to exchange supplies on the night Dad and Ottie encountered them.

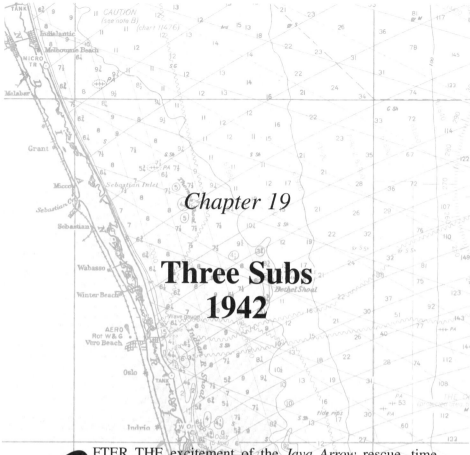

Chapter 19

Three Subs
1942

FTER THE excitement of the *Java Arrow* rescue, time passed slowly for the *Kitsis* and her volunteer crew. As summer progressed, the days turned hotter. Late afternoon thunderstorms from towering cumulus clouds, generated inland, moved eastward to drench the coastal communities. West winds blowing off the land left the sea calm. Offshore, Ottie and Kit watched the shadows of freighters and tankers, now with Navy and Coast Guard escorts, passing by. Ottie read in the paper about a ship blowing up off New Orleans. He figured the subs must have moved into the Gulf of Mexico, because they sure weren't along the Florida coast. He hadn't heard of a ship being sunk in weeks. The rumor was that the Coast Guard would soon cease sending Coast Guard Auxiliary boats out along the East Coast.

On the evening of July 17, 1942, Ottie and Kit reported to the Lieutenant at the Fort Pierce Coast Guard Station as usual, who told them, "I want you boys to go out on another boat tonight. It's loading out at the dock right now. The owner isn't familiar with the waters around Bethel Shoal, and you all are."

They walked to the dock. Two Navy seamen and another man, whom the Lieutenant introduced as Ed, were wrestling a piece of radio equipment into the cockpit of his 40-foot Elco. Ed, a short man with brown hair wearing his rubber boots, looked like he might have been a commercial fisherman.

Ed explained what was going on. "These Navy fellows came down from Banana River Naval Air Station at Cape Canaveral with the radio gear in a truck. We're to sit off Bethel Shoal. They're going to give us air cover tonight, and these guys are supposed to keep in touch with the planes."

"Air cover? We hardly ever see or hear a plane out there at night," remarked Kit. He took out his bottle of Amphojel, took a swig, and put it in his back pocket.

"Well, I don't know. That's all they told me," replied Ed.

"This sure seems peculiar," Ottie commented.

"We've got this radio. Maybe we can use it as a depth charge, but on what I don't know," said Ed, giving the radio rack a final shove into place. "You guys pretty good with a line? Tie her down."

Ottie grabbed a coil of rope off the deck, and he and Kit guyed the radio so if any kind of sea came up, it wouldn't topple. Ed started the engine; the seamen handled the lines. As dusk settled, they headed out the inlet. Once outside, Ed turned the wheel over to Kit. The sea lay quiet. Darkness came quickly. There was no moon and the stars blinked sharply. Ottie relieved Kit for the last half-hour and steered by the North Star. They passed several miles offshore from Vero Beach, and Ottie thought they were near where they had picked up the *Java Arrow* crew two months earlier.

Ottie hit Bethel Shoal on the nose — pretty good navigating for a dark night, he thought. The buoy light had been extinguished since May — after all the ships had been sunk — but they could hear its whistle as it rocked several hundred feet off the bow. Kit threw the anchor over and Ottie cut the engine. Ed said they had been instructed to lay there until dawn. Meanwhile, the Navy boys had the radio emitting a beep every 30 seconds. They didn't talk much, but Ottie guessed that the Banana River Naval Air Station must be monitoring their position.

Kit and Ed took the first watch; Ottie went below for a snooze and drifted off quickly. It seemed only minutes later that he heard a commotion on the deck above. He jumped out of the bunk and hurried up into the cockpit. The Navy seamen were down on the deck, one talking into the radio in a frantic whisper. Ed stood at the controls trying to fire up the engine. Kit kneeled on the bow as he pulled up the anchor. He pointed.

Ahead, not more than 25 yards, Ottie saw the black mass of a surfaced submarine. The silhouette of the conning tower was unmistakable. The sound of idling diesels rumbled across the water. Ottie's stomach cramped; bile flowed into his mouth.

"Jesus, God," he exclaimed. He stood frozen, staring at the black mass on the water.

The roar of the boat's engine broke Ottie's trance. Ed swung the rudder hard to starboard. Kit hollered, "Look out!"

Ahead, Ottie saw the black shapes of two more subs laying side by side. Ed spun the wheel back, threw the throttle full forward knocking Ottie off balance, and headed toward shore at full power. Kit came back into the cockpit; he and Ottie stared at the black forms now off the stern. The Navy boys squatted, staying as low as they could. One gripped the microphone and pleaded over the radio as if praying for a plane to materialize instantly overhead.

As the boat ran, kicking up a white wake, two of the subs disappeared into the blackness, but they could still see one. Suddenly from her conning tower a light blinked.

Kit exclaimed, "They're signaling us. What the hell's going on?"

"It looks like they're coming after us," replied Ottie.

"Christ, I hope not! They can outrun us. Get down!"

"Why would they chase us?" asked Ottie as they crouched, trying to duck below the transom. "One burst from that gun on the conning tower and we'd be goners."

Ottie poked his head up to peer at the monstrous conning tower closing on them. He could still hear the sub's diesels despite the noise of their own engine.

Ottie frantically tied his life jacket. He told Kit, "I'm going over the side. I'd rather be floating around in the middle of the ocean than end up in Germany."

"No you don't, God-damn it! We'll take our chances with the boat." Kit shouted, grabbing Ottie by the arm.

Kit let go and dashed across the cockpit and spoke to Ed who stood totally exposed at the wheel. He hollered above the noise of the boat's engine, "We can't outrun 'em. We've got to outmaneuver the bastards. Turn her sharp. Zigzag. Running straight, we're gone."

Ottie saw Ed spin the wheel, turning the boat to port so she ran at right angles to the sub. He looked at the sub broadside, all 200 feet of her, as she began to swing to their course. Ed turned back to starboard. Ottie raised his head just enough to see over the side. The sub started falling behind. Ottie stared at the gun mounted on a platform behind the conning tower. He could see the silhouettes of two men manning it. He waited in terror for the darkness to be ripped apart by fire.

Ed changed course several times, swinging sharply, rolling Ottie off his haunches and onto the deck and gaining distance with each maneuver. The sub disappeared into the darkness.

Ottie, soaked with sweat, stood up. "Have we lost her?" he said to no one.

Ed now had the boat hugging the beach, just outside the surf, heading north toward Cape Canaveral and the safety of the Banana River Naval Air Station. They could see the white phosphorous of the small waves breaking on the shore. Ottie looked ahead for the rotating beacon of the lighthouse on the Cape. Then he realized it also had been extinguished in May.

Kit asked one of the radiomen, "What the hell happened to the air cover?"

"Don't know," he replied. "Banana River told us to keep reporting our position and where the subs were."

"Big help that was!" grumbled Kit.

"What were those subs doing there?" asked Ottie.

"Must have been exchanging supplies and charging their batteries," answered Kit. "Three of them sitting side by side. That's crazy."

Ottie relieved Ed at the wheel and steered the boat. At daybreak, he saw the silhouette of the Banana River Air Base water tower on the island. Ahead just beyond the quiet surf lay a Coast Guard lifeboat waiting for them. The instructions from the radio were for Kit and Ottie to come ashore and brief the Navy on what they had seen. Ed, the two sailors, and the radio equipment were to proceed north to Ponce Inlet at New Smyrna where the sailors and their radio equipment were to be picked up.

The lifeboat came alongside, Ottie and Kit climbed aboard, and two Coast Guardsmen rowed them the 30 yards to shore. A Navy jeep that had been waiting on the beach took them on a brief ride to a gray, single-story building. Ottie saw only three or four other buildings — one a hangar — all sitting on a strip of bare sand dunes between the ocean and the Banana

River. Except for the surrounding water the place looked like an outpost in the Sahara Desert.

A sailor with a .45-caliber pistol in a holster on a web belt escorted them into the building and led them into a room with a couple of desks and some chairs. Silhouettes of submarines were tacked to the wall. A lieutenant and an ensign joined them.

"I understand you guys had a scare last night," stated the Lieutenant.

"Yea. Where were the planes?" asked Kit.

"Sorry, but our aircraft availability is not your concern."

"We could have been machine-gunned by those guys or captured and on our way to Germany," remarked Ottie.

"Let me ask you some questions," suggested the Lieutenant. "Look at these silhouettes. Do any of them resemble the subs you saw last night?"

Ottie and Kit looked and agreed that one of the subs seemed to have a conning tower forward on her superstructure. Kit and Ottie's choice baffled the officers.

"Are you sure?" one of them asked. "That's an Italian submarine."

"Looked like it to me," replied Kit. Ottie nodded.

The officers asked about the subs' maneuverability, about their guns, about how many men they had seen on deck, and about the sound of their engines.

Kit interrupted. "How fast can those subs run?"

"Fast enough," said the Lieutenant. The officers then cut off the conversation, shook hands with Kit and Ottie, and suggested they go over to the mess and eat breakfast before they were flown back to the Coast Guard Station at Fort Pierce.

After eggs, bacon, and two cups each of black coffee, Kit and Ottie were escorted out to the seaplane ramp. They passed the open door of the hangar and saw two planes with the cowlings off the engines undergoing repair.

"Maybe that's why we didn't see planes last night," cracked Kit.

On the ramp, a seaplane rested on wheels that protruded from the underneath pontoon, with its single engine idling. It had a long cockpit, a pontoon the length of its fuselage, and a small pontoon at the tip of each wing. Ottie recognized the observation plane, from pictures he had seen, as the OSU Kingfisher used on battleships and cruisers and launched by catapult. He wondered how the Navy was going to use this type of plane to attack submarines. It looked as if Banana River Naval Air Station's total complement of aircraft consisted of these six clumsy-looking planes.

The young pilot shook hands with Kit and Ottie and waved them up the ladder into the cockpit. They squeezed into two seats, one behind the other, in back of the pilot. After they had helped him push the canopy forward over their heads, he gunned the engine and taxied down the ramp into the slick waters of the Banana River. Spray shot up on either side of the cockpit and the canopy rattled as the plane roared down the river and finally lifted off the water. Ottie, who was sitting behind Kit, turned his head and saw the air base and, beyond, the beach curving seaward to form Cape Canaveral.

Flying at what Ottie guessed was about 100 mph, they passed at an altitude of 1,000 feet over the narrow tip of Merritt Island where the Banana and Indian Rivers joined, and the plane headed south down the wide expanse of water. The small town of Melbourne went by beneath the right wing. Then Ottie saw the Sebastian Inlet which normally cut through the narrow island to the river but was now filling with sand from lack of dredging.

With Vero Beach ahead, he looked out to sea toward Bethel Shoal where they had seen the subs. The sun sparkled off the ocean, and he saw what he thought might be an oil slick. He tapped Kit on the shoulder in front of him and pointed. Kit nodded. Had the Navy indeed sunk one of the subs? They would never know.

The plane passed over the wooden bridges crossing the river at Wabasso and Winter Beach, and Ottie could see the Vero bridge ahead. He spotted the tin roof of the Vero Beach city dock reflecting the sun, saw the Riomar golf course by the beach on his left. He turned his head and looked toward the mainland and saw the open expanse of the Vero airport and the town next to it. He could see the land being cleared for the new Naval Air Station.

A few minutes later, the pilot swung the plane in over downtown Fort Pierce, and approaching from the west, lined up on the inlet and landed the Kingfisher in a running spray of water. Ottie watched as they flashed by a small boat, tied to a buoy, with two men fishing. The plane taxied to the ramp at the Coast Guard Station. Ottie and Kit crawled out of the cockpit, told the pilot goodbye, and walked over to the main building. There they were interrogated for an hour by two officers, one of whom they knew. As they were being questioned, Ottie felt like he and Kit must be the only people on the east coast of Florida who had ever seen a German submarine.

With the questioning over, they got in Kit's Model A and headed for home. As they crossed the bridge into Fort Pierce, Ottie dozed off.

Two weeks later, the Navy flew Kit Johnson to Pensacola Naval Air Station to brief the Admiral about the encounter with the subs. Ottie figured the Admiral wanted to talk to someone who had seen the real thing.

Chapter 20

The Man He Was
1990

*T*HE CALL CAME at 9:30 p.m. Time had passed since I had returned from Germany, and I was back in the routine, had come off the euphoria of my visit with Peter, and was buried in work, trying to keep the Saudi project with the Dutch and the Koreans on schedule. I was sitting on the glassed-in back porch dozing with the newspaper spread across my lap. Katharine was watching *Murphy Brown* on TV.

I got up from my chair and went into the kitchen, reaching the phone on the third ring.

"Rody, it's Sue."

She didn't have to tell me. Her voice was unmistakable — Mom and Dad's nurse. These calls, especially at night, generally meant that Mom had had an emphysema attack and that we were probably headed cross-state to Shell Point. Over the years, Mom's smoking had ruined her lungs. An attack meant she would be on her way to a hospital. Recovery from these attacks was now taking weeks. At times, we had driven to Fort Myers not knowing whether she would be alive when we arrived.

"It's Kit," said Sue. "He has a temperature of 104 degrees, his lungs are congested, he has diarrhea, his stools are black."

Not Mom this time, I thought. Dad rarely had health problems, other than Alzheimer's, that is. "How long has he had this?"

"The temperature, a couple of days, but it's worse now. I'm going to stay with him tonight. There's been a Staph infection on the floor. I think you should come." Sue rarely asked that we come; she let us make that decision ourselves.

I asked her if Mom knew.

"No. She's still so frail," Sue replied.

"OK, we're on our way." I hung up and walked back out on the porch.

"Who called?" asked Katharine, glancing away from the TV.

"It was Sue. Dad's not doing well."

"Dad?" She got up from the couch. "What's the matter?"

I told her.

"You're so tired tonight. Does she think we should go over there?"

"She even asked that we come."

"Let's go," she said.

I found a suitcase, and we stuffed some things in it. Katharine called a neighbor to ask her to take care of the dogs. When she hung up, she suggested, "You know we should get smart and keep a bag packed."

On one of the other trips we had packed the bag and then driven off and left it. This time we grabbed the suitcase. I checked my wallet and had 50 dollars. The car had half a tank of gas which would get us to Okeechobee, where I knew we could get more gas no matter how late it was.

We drove in silence south to Fort Pierce and then west on Route 70. The road was straight; there was no traffic; a half moon partially illuminated the flat cattle land. I drove as if in a daze. I was tired but felt that somehow God was pulling the car down the dark road, the headlights tracking the white center line. My only fear was a deer bounding across in front us.

"What are you thinking?" asked Katharine.

"Nothing." I didn't want to talk. I never wanted to talk in these situations. I had been thinking that Mom had always been the one who had given us these scares, not Dad, yet he had been in the Pavilion for years. He had deteriorated physically and could no longer walk, but except for an occasional cold, his health had been good. I suppose that was because he had such good care with Sue, Jean, and his other nurses.

Dad's worst time had been the first few months after he had been put into the Pavilion. The doctors tried different drugs to calm him down. Instead, the drugs tore him up, as if he had a war going on in his head. I could see it in his face; he twisted his mouth, his eyes shot back and forth, he kept putting his hands to his head, he shook his head in torment. Watching him made me want to cry. Then the doctors stopped the drugs, and he became his old docile, gentle self. He never gave his nurses any more problems, well almost no problems. I smiled as I remembered some of the funny things Sue and Jean told us about him.

Worried about his fellow patients being tied into their wheel chairs, Dad, using his nautical knowledge of knots, played a Robin Hood role and took great pleasure in releasing them. For this, he was tied in his chair.

On another occasion, Pappy became concerned about his roommate, Mr. Herzog, when he saw a tube hanging out of Mr. Herzog's penis. Dad slipped out of bed and in some manner removed the catheter. The next morning, Mr. Herzog's nurse discovered what had happened to her patient. She was not pleased and accosted Sue with, "There was some bleeding."

"What do you expect? Do you think Kit went to med school?" replied Sue.

Another time, Sue told us Dad had been standing at the wash basin, looking into the mirror, just talking away. The only decipherable word Sue could hear was "Howard," and he repeated it several times. Sue said, "Kit was having a conversation with Howard. They were pretty close, weren't they?"

"Yes, amazingly so," I replied.

But the story that tickled me the most was the one about the aquarium. Sue was walking Dad through the Pavilion waiting room with its upholstered chairs, couch, flowers in vases on the end tables, reception desk, and a TV. Near the entrance to the room sat a large aquarium. The residents fed the fish. Sue stopped so Dad could watch the fish. A small typewritten message was scotch taped on the glass. It read: "If you overfeed, you will kill the fish."

At this point, Dad could still comprehend writing and peering through his bifocals he perused the sign. Then, he said in a voice that could be heard throughout the lobby, "Kill the bastards."

And so I told Katharine that I was thinking about the funny things that Dad had done.

"Thank goodness there has been something to laugh about," she said. We sat in silence for a minute or two, the wind whistling over the car as we sped down the highway, then she remarked, "You know the best thing that could happen to Dad is if he would go."

"I know that." What I knew was that Katharine was trying to prepare me for what might come.

We drove on. At 11 p.m., I turned the car into the brightly lit gas pumps outside the Circle K convenience store just north of Okeechobee. I started a pump and Katharine got out of the car and took the gas nozzle from my hand. "Why don't you go call?" she suggested.

I walked across the lot to the pay phones. The last time I had used this phone was three or four months ago when Mom had been taken from Shell Point to the emergency room at Lee Memorial Hospital in Fort Myers. They had put her on a ventilator which did the breathing for her.

I punched in the phone and credit card numbers, and the floor nurse answered. I asked her to switch me to Dad's room. Sue answered.

"How is Dad?" I asked.

"Doing better. His temperature is down to 102."

"We'll be there in a couple of hours."

"I'll be here," she replied.

I hung up and walked back to the car. Katharine had just finished filling the tank. She looked at me.

"He's holding his own," I said.

"Good!"

At 1:30 a.m., we drove in through the gate at Shell Point and went directly to the Pavilion. We walked down the quiet hallways and took the elevator to the third floor. The last part of the drive had gone by quickly. Katharine told me about a Dick Francis novel that she had just read. At least, it stopped me from thinking about Dad.

Sue was sitting next to Dad's bed. She stood up. "He's doing better."

I walked to his bed. An oxygen mask covered his face. He breathed heavily with gasps, his mouth open. We stayed for 20 minutes, then Sue sent us off to a nearby motel. We asked her to call if he got worse.

At 7:30 the next morning, we were back in his room. Sue had gone home to sleep, and Jean, his other long-time nurse, was there. Dad was stable, his temperature normal, and the oxygen mask was gone. "He's a tough old bird," Jean remarked.

We went down to the first floor to see Mom where she had been for several weeks after her last bout with emphysema. Her small frame made her look like a child in the bed, despite her gray hair and the oxygen tube running to her nose. I put my hand on her wrist with its purple blotches and it felt like bare bone through the loose skin. She recognized us with a weak smile. I kissed her forehead. She spoke, but I couldn't make out her words. Katharine and I told her the news of the children, but she didn't respond. I couldn't tell how much she understood. She dozed off and we left.

I went to find Dad's doctor. He was in his office on a wing of the Pavilion. He sat behind his desk; I stood.

I said, "I don't think we need to keep giving my dad antibiotics. He has a living will." The doctor nodded.

I continued. "I think you know how my mother felt. She has said many times, 'Give Kit the best care possible, but let nature take its course.'"

"Yes, Mr. Johnson. We will follow your wishes. The medicine will be stopped." He took a pen and made a note on Dad's chart which lay on his desk. He looked up, "You know, of course, your father could shake this infection on his own and live several years."

"I appreciate that," I said. "I just want him to be as comfortable as possible as long as he lives."

The doctor answered that he understood. I extended my hand; the doctor stood and shook it. I left his office and walked back to the Pavilion along the water's edge. My feelings were torn. I had struggled with this decision for some time. Katharine and I had talked about it, and what I might face when the time came. That time seemed to be now. How could I stop something that might keep my dad alive? On the other hand, what kind of life did he have? He had now been in the Pavilion for nine years. But he wasn't in pain; he had no comprehension of his situation. So?

I had been through the living will thing with Mom. Once she had been taken to the hospital emergency room. A doctor, not knowing her, had put her on a ventilator so she could breathe. Katharine and I had been told that the shock to the system of coming off a ventilator could kill a person as well, especially if they were not strong. Mom's regular doctor, knowing her wishes and about her living will, would have made her comfortable, and "let nature take its course." That was a year before. She had had some quality of life since, seen her grandchildren and great-grand daughters, even spent a weekend with us over on Sanibel Island across the bay. I wasn't sure what was right, but I felt Dad's life ought to be under the control of God, not some doctor.

I went back upstairs to be with Pappy by myself. His eyes were closed, he gripped a small, soft stuffed dog close to his chest, his silvery hair was pushed back above his ears, his complexion was almost white except for brown splotches on his skin. His mouth hung slack. He breathed easier. His legs were pulled up, and he seemed very short. His hands still had strength, but his arm muscles were flabby and felt soft to my touch. I rubbed his arms wanting to be connected in some way. He was fresh and clean and smelled good, not like the hallway with its penetrating odors of urine and disinfectant from the other Alzheimer's patients, who were up and milling around.

In Dad's room on the wall at the foot of his bed was a portrait of me done by Katharine that Mom liked. On Dad's table by his bed, sitting among bottles of medicine and lotions, was a colored, miniature picture of him in his Coast Guard uniform. The nurses had put it there, Jean had commented, "as a reminder of the man he was." These were his only possessions. I kissed him on the top of his head, looked up, and prayed, "Dear God, please take him." I left the room.

A couple of months later, the Indian River County Historical Society found out that I had made the trip to Germany the year before and asked me to give a presentation at their monthly meeting about World War II U-boat activity off Vero Beach. I would talk about Kit Johnson, Ottie Roach, Peter Cremer, the *Kitsis*, the *Java Arrow*, *U-333*, and the three subs. The evening before the talk, I appeared on a local cable television channel to publicize the event. The TV studio was small. The chair felt hard, the lights blinded me, and their heat baked my forehead. Perspiration ran down my cheeks. At a desk sat the pretty TV host, smiling as she asked me questions. I told her about my father and showed the TV cameras a picture of the *Kitsis*. She looked at me earnestly, and said, "Well, your father was a hero, wasn't he?"

I froze. Tears came to my eyes. Something snapped into place. I finally knew the answer.

"Yes, my father was a hero."

Afterword

In Memory

Howard S. Johnson	1906-1979
Ottie Roach	1908-1991
Peter Cremer Thursby	1911-1992
Florence (Sis) A. Johnson	1913-1994
Clarence (Kit) B. Johnson	1906-1995

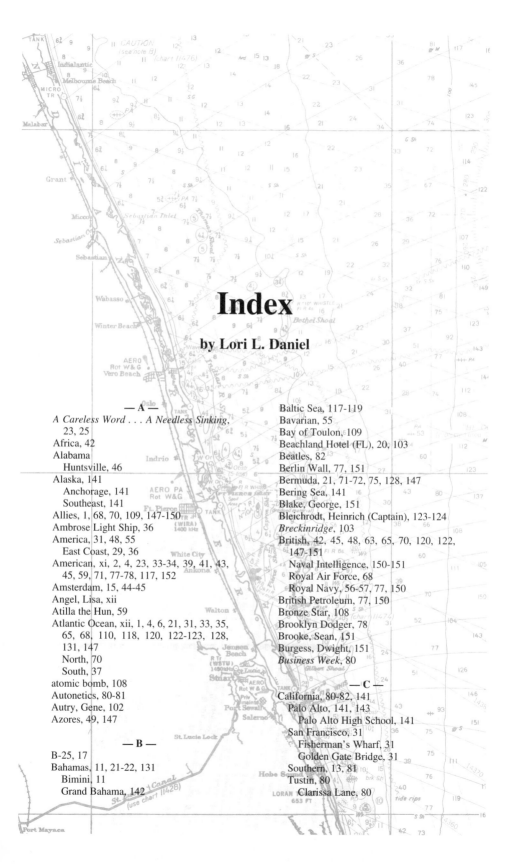

Index

by Lori L. Daniel